COMMON SENSE CAREGIVING

Promoting Humane Caregiving of Elderly Parents

Dr. Mary Ellen Erickson

Illustrations on the cover by Julie Haberman

Mary Ellen Erickson
180 90th Avenue SE
Kensal, ND 58455

COMMON SENSE CAREGIVING

Promoting Humane Caregiving of Elderly Parents

Copyright © 2004 by Dr. Mary Ellen Erickson

First edition ~ 2004

Printed in the United States of America

Contents

Personal Observations   1

Acknowledgments   3

Introduction   4

Part I   6
  Chapter 1: Why Do Caregiving?   7
  Chapter 2: It's All About Attitude!   12

Part II   16
  Chapter 3: Motivation   17
  Chapter 4: Roles and Tasks   23
  Chapter 5: Family Relationships   34
  Chapter 6: Personality Changes and Growth   46

Part III   59
  Chapter 7: Strategies or Adaptations   61

Part IV   81
  Chapter 8: Religion or Spirituality   83
  Chapter 9: Institutionalization   92

Part V   111
  Chapter 10: Positive Aspects of Caregiving   113
  Chapter 11: Making the Decision   122

Resources   127

Appendix   128

Personal Observations

This book grew out of the experiences and information obtained when I wrote a dissertation for a Ph.D. in human services for Walden University. After completion of the Ph.D., the next logical step was to share with caregivers the information and knowledge I obtained, while doing my dissertation.

My husband and I had been involved with caregiving of elderly parents intermittently from 1976 to 1997. Our mothers were both in their 60s when they died of cancer, and our fathers were both in their 80s when they died of complications brought on by old age. My feelings during the years of caregiving left me wondering how others felt when in this situation. Feelings of pride and accomplishment for a job well done were primary when the caregiving was completed; however, other feelings of frustration, guilt, stress, and burden were sometimes present during the caregiving experience. In an effort to sort out my own feelings about caregiving and be of possible help to others that will go through this experience, I decided to do my dissertation on caregiving of elderly parents by adult children.

Most of the literature researched for the dissertation was on negative aspects of caregiving. What was needed was a project on positive aspects of caregiving to motivate the caregiver to be steadfast and acquire all the benefits that caregiving can bring. With this thought in mind, I set out on a two-year journey to discover and record positive aspects of caregiving as seen through the eyes of those who had been through the experience.

The premise of this book is that the real experts on caregiving are those who have experienced it first hand. Because of this premise, I have used some of the dialogue from the interviews to paint a picture of successful caregiving for my readers. I have interpreted and synthesized

1

the interviews and added narrative to provide an outline that will help the reader understand the process of successful caregiving. I have used my own experiences and learned knowledge to introduce, clarify, and summarize each chapter of this book.

 If you want to achieve a positive attitude about caregiving of elders, read this book. You may laugh, you may cry, but you will come away from this read with new insights into how to take care of your elderly parents in a humane way that will gain you the respect of your siblings, peers, community, children, and most of all your elderly parents. Best of all, you will respect yourself for having done *the best job you could possible do.*

Acknowledgments

Caregiving in rural America has been passed down from generation to generation. This fact was prominent in the interviews done for this book. Many thanks to the fifteen couples in Foster County, North Dakota that I interviewed for this study. They gave me several hours of their time filling out questionnaires and telling their stories with sincerity and humor. They are part of the larger network of "Caregiving Heroes" across our country.

Special thanks to my husband and best friend, Dwayne, for hanging in there with me through this whole ordeal. Thanks also to Dr. William Barkley, my committee chairman and mentor, for turning a farmer's wife into a scholar.

This book is dedicated in memory of Alice and Andreas Christmann and Mabel and Gust Erickson, wonderful parents and in-laws. Without their love, none of this would have been possible.

Introduction

Common Sense Caregiving is written for adult children who are or may be doing caregiving of an elderly parent. The intent of this book is to motivate any caregivers of elders to take on this challenge with a positive attitude. Looking at caregiving from a positive view will make the experience more rewarding and help promote personal growth and psychological well-being in the individual that undertakes this endeavor.

Common Sense Caregiving is divided into five parts:

• Part 1 explains you why you should do caregiving and discusses the importance of a positive attitude.

• Part 2 outlines the important factors to consider for positive caregiving results.

• Part 3 discusses coping strategies that can be used to become a successful caregiver.

• Part 4 considers the religious/spiritual aspects of caregiving and how to institutionalize elders when other options are exhausted.

• Part 5 summarizes the positive aspects of caregiving and provides a final argument to motive family members to take care of their elders.

Definitions

Some definitions and qualifications are necessary to set the stage for your understand of this book. These are listed according to appearance in the book.

Caregiving: A process of providing assistance to a frail elder on a regular basis.

Caregiver: A person who provides non-ordinary help to any elderly person who is experiencing mental or physical failure.

Care Recipient: A frail elder who needs help with a least one ADL or IADL function on a regular basis.

Activities of Daily Living (ADL): Activities of help provided by caregivers such as bathing, eating, dressing, toileting, getting around, and other skills necessary for daily survival.

Instrumental Activities of Daily Living (IADL): Activities provided by caregivers that include physical, financial, and/or emotional support necessary at given times.

Religion: A particular system of beliefs or faith in a supreme being and worship of that supreme being.

Spirituality: The inner human spirit that can affect how religion is practiced.

Moral Reasoning: The ability to make decisions that are morally acceptable when moral conflict arises. Moral reasoning involves more other-concerns than self-concerns. Moral reasoning is doing the right thing because of moral righteousness rather than solving problems with the easiest solutions.

Nursing home: Any institution that takes care of elderly people. This care can range from basic care to intensive care.

Attitude: A readiness to respond favorably or unfavorably to a person, situation, or event.

Common Sense: A form of decision making that is unselfish, understandable, and practical.

Quotations

Most of the quotes used in this book came from the individuals interviewed for the research study. Some of these quotes were altered slightly to promote better understanding for the reader. These individuals choose to remain anonymous. Those requests will be honored.

PART I

PAINTING NOW THE PICTURE
By Edwin W. Truesdell

When my hair is thin and silvered,
And my time of toil is through;
When I've many years behind me,
And ahead of me a few;
I shall want to sit, I reckon,
Sort of dreaming in the sun;
And recall the roads I've traveled
And the many things I've done.

I hope there'll be no picture
That I'll hate to look upon;
When the time to paint is better
Or to wipe it out, is gone.
I hope there'll be no vision
Of a hasty word I've said
That has left a trail of sorrow,
Like a whip welt sore and red.

And I hope my old age dreaming
Will bring back no bitter scene
Of a time when I was selfish,
Or a time when I was mean.
When I'm getting old and feeble,
And I'm far along life's way,
I don't want to sit regretting any bygone yesterday.

I am painting now the picture
That I'll want someday to see;
I am filling in a canvas
That will soon come back to me.
Though nothing great is on it,
And though nothing there is fine,
I shall want to look it over
When I'm old and call it mine.
So I do not dare to leave it
While the paint is warm and wet,
With a single thing upon it
That I later will regret.

"They needed help so we helped them.
Isn't that what people are supposed to do?"

Chapter 1

Why Do Caregiving?

Chapter Goal: To outline the reasons for doing caregiving for elderly parents.

Some people in our society think that caregiving of frail, elderly parents is a natural process that all children will want to undertake when the time comes. We know this was not always true in the past and is certainly not always true today. Many past and present circumstances will prevent adult children from taking care of their elderly parents. Could these adult children be persuaded to help their elderly parents if they had more knowledge of the caregiving experience? Would putting a positive spin on the caregiving experience motivate adult children to provide care for frail elders? I feel the answer to these two questions is "yes."

Betty Kramer in her 1997 journal article, "Gain in the caregiving experience: Where are we? What next?" discusses the need for caregivers to understand the positive aspects of caregiving and share those experiences with others. Kramer suggests that all caregivers could provide better care if they were more knowledgeable on how to do better caregiving. She also believes that discussing positive caregiving experiences with others will give more meaning to these caregiving experiences, which in some cases requires a great deal of sacrifice over a long period of time.

I agree with Ms. Kramer's suggestions. In the interviews I did with the fifteen couples that provided information for this book, I discovered they all wanted to talk about their experiences and put a positive spin on caregiving. They also wanted to encourage others to do caregiving because they had received so many reward and blessings from the caregiving they had done through the years. The couples were all happy to share their knowledge on caregiving and readily agreed to let me write about our interviews so that others would have the information it took them years to learn.

How has caregiving changed in the past century?
The majority of the population was rural at the beginning of the twentieth century. Families were large and there were always chores to do. Elders could remain useful well into old age in the family system by performing simple household tasks, helping with child care, or assisting with outdoor farm chores.

Elders did not live as long at the beginning of the twentieth century. When elders became incapacitated, their families took care of them until they passed away. Since medication was not as effective and other health services were not as efficient as they are now, elders who became seriously ill did not live very long.

Deborah Stone in her 1999 article, "Care and Trembling," describes how caregiving in the late twentieth century has *gone public.* Women in the workplace is one contributing factor for more public elder care. Caregiving, especially for the oldest-old, has become a business for profit. Much of this care is now paid for by public subsidies, tax credits, exemptions, insurance companies, and the care recipients or children of the recipients. Stone believes that when caregiving becomes public, it is depleted of "emotional force and spiritual meaning because the bottom line becomes profit." According to Stone, "when caregiving becomes public, losses in altruism, generosity, and cooperation potentials for families of the care recipients are inevitable." Stone also feels that the nursing homes cannot provide care with the same moral standards as those given by family members.

I agree with Ms. Stone. What needs to be done is to combine the older ideologies (attitudes) on caregiving with the newer technologies (technical devices, medicines, and services) in caregiving. A home based elder care system, using the newest technologies, with a loving family member in charge would be the best form of elder care available. The attitudes of older caregivers promoted in this book stress the positive aspects of caregiving by focusing on emotional forces and spiritual meanings. Acquiring these attitudes will help caregivers provide the most humane treatment for their elders.

Has our society changed?

The demographics, lifestyles, and technologies in our society have changed, but the ideology on who should do the caregiving has not changed. Society still expects adult children to take care of their elderly parents.

Recent population demographics show that families are getting smaller. Because there are fewer siblings to take care of their elderly parents, the patterns of caregiving will change. Sibling mobility has increased with improved transportation, job opportunities, and a more independent, well-educated young population. Changing demographics will create the question of *"Who will remain at home to take care of elderly parents?"*

Four lifestyle factors that have promoted new caregiving problems in our present society are more women working, more divorces, more single- parent homes, and more remarried couples. With more women working in full-time jobs away from the home, caregiving duties must be shared with a spouse (or significant other) to relieve the stress and burden that will evolve if a woman tries to work a full-time job and do primary caregiving for an elderly parent at the same time. Partners who understand each other's needs and are supportive are essential in successful caregiving.

In the past most married couples had the same sets of childhood parents and in-law parents throughout their adult life. This promoted very close relationships that involved love, respect, and concern. Because of these close relationships, in-laws were taken care of in the same manner as childhood parents. Changing family structures will change this family dynamic.

As couples divorce and remarry, in-laws often become sources of conflict because new spouses need to compete with former spouses for the affection and respect needed for successful caregiving. Relationships in remarriages can also become very complicated with extended family members who are necessary for successful caregiving.

Individuals who are single (divorced, widowed, or never married) have problems when caregiving becomes so demanding that it interferes with employment. If these single individuals do not have shared caregiving duties with some other adult (a sibling, extended family, public service provider) they will not be able to continue full-time employment which can affect their present financial situation and their future retirement benefits.

Another lifestyle change in our society that affects present day caregiving is the *sandwiched* couples. These couples married later in life and had children when they were older. *Sandwiched* couples are those who take care of children at the same time they take care of elders. This can sometimes be a very difficult situation involving living space, finances, and discipline of the children.

Many *sandwiched* couples will be working full-time when they are called upon to do elder caregiving. This situation will impact our society in a number of ways. They will be absent from work more often; they may start doing part-time employment or take early retirement, which will affect their pensions; and their productivity may decline because of all the stress and burden they will face.

Our society has changed. *Who will take care of our elders? How will our elders be cared for? Where will our elders get the care they need?* These are all good questions we need to answer in the twenty first century.

Why is modeling important?

Modeling is a very important factor needed to pass tradition from one generation to another. Frances Goldscheider and Leora Lawton in a 1998 journal article, *"Family experiences and the erosion of support for inter-generational co-residence,"* suggest that children raised with grandparents living in their homes are more open to this way of living when the time comes to take care of their own parents. I found this to be true when I interviewed the fifteen couples for my study. Most adults will not try some living arrangement they have never experienced or have heard much negative information about.

What is the normal life cycle process?

A renowned developmentalist, Erik Erikson, proposed eight stages of life cycle development. He suggested that individuals in the final stage of the life cycle needed to develop integrity before they die, or they would spend their final years in a state of despair. It would seem to me that no generation of a society could develop integrity by neglecting the elders in their society ~ especially if those elders are their parents.

When discussing feelings with the fifteen couples interviewed for this book, some mentioned feelings of guilt. If some of these couples, who had done everything possible for their elders over long periods of time, had some feelings of guilt, imagine the amount of guilt that will be felt by adult children who do nothing to help their frail, elderly parents. Guilty feelings can certainly lead to feelings of despair in old age. Once the frail elder has passed on, it is too late to make up for the neglect and lack of concern shown for that elderly parent's needs.

The human life cycle, which starts with childhood and continues all the way to old-age, is a normal process for all individuals to go through. We need to develop and mature physically and mentally in each of the other seven stages of our life cycle to reach the final stage. This last stage can lead to integrity by passing through the first seven stages successfully. Integrity in the final stage of life is needed for peace of mind as an individual contemplates his or her own mortality in old age.

Summation

The verdict? Caregiving of elderly parents is a necessary activity in any human life cycle. If you want to learn how to achieve a positive attitude about caregiving continue reading this book. You may feel better or worse when you finish, but you will come away from this read with new insight into how to take care of your elderly parents in a humane way that will gain you the respect of your siblings, peers, community, children, and most of all your elderly parents. Best of all, you will respect yourself for having done *the best job you could possibly do.*

Chapter Chuckle

You know you are getting older when . . .
- Everything hurts and what doesn't hurt, doesn't work.
- You feel like the night before, and you haven't been anywhere.
- Your little black book contains only names ending in M.D.

"I guess my attitude is that there is a time and a season ~
this is meant to be ~ this is life ~ old age ~ just accept it.
It's part of the process. We are going through this together.
It isn't abnormal; it's just the life-process!"

Chapter 2

It's All About Attitude!

Chapter Goal: To outline seven categories for successful caregiving and the attitudes involved in each category.

The quotation at the beginning of this chapter was spoken with passion to communicate the idea that attitude is an important factor in successful caregiving. Every couple I interviewed mentioned that having a good attitude was very important for successful caregiving. Since I interviewed married couples together, some of my responses will refer to couples, but the answers were always given by an individual expressing their personal opinion, even though the spouse was listening to the response. Most spouses were in total agreement on answers to questions. Since these couples had been married from 30 to 48 years, they knew each other very well.

Some people are born with a positive outlook in all aspects of their lives, others need to learn how to be positive about different aspects of life. I had no idea if the people I interviewed were born with positive attitudes or had achieved those attitudes throughout their life cycle. I do know that they all had positive attitudes which lead to successful caregiving experiences. Since the focus of my study was on positive attitudes, I chose only couples that I felt would have a positive attitude ~ none of them disappointed me. *How did I know they would have a positive attitude toward the caregiving they had done?* Because they agreed to be interviewed and share their most intimate thoughts with me. I thought that people who had only negative experiences with caregiving would not want to share those feelings with a stranger. I was right.

What makes couples successful at caregiving?
I condensed the findings from my interviews into seven categories. Each category tells what is needed to be a successful caregiver. The attitudes needed to achieve success in that category are also outlined. All seven of these categories will be discussed in more detail in the next seven chapters.

1. *Successful couple caregivers* are motivated by the same factors as other caregivers: affection, responsibility, reciprocity, expectations of elders, obligation, and religion/spirituality.

The attitudes needed to be motivated by these factors included: appreciation, pride, self-esteem, integrity, patience, knowledge of human nature, a sense of belonging, a sense of accomplishment, a sense of importance, and a strong religious faith or spirituality. These attitudes may have been instilled in the caregivers by the people they were taking care of. **Reader take note:** *Being a good parent may assure you that your children will want to take care of you when you become old and frail.*

2. *Successful couple caregivers* have clearly defined roles and flexibility in their work schedules, thinking, and lifestyle.

The attitudes needed to accomplish the tasks and successfully perform the roles of caregiving include empathy, cooperation, a good work ethic, understanding of others feelings, the ability to change, and the ability to sacrifice. By doing mostly traditional tasks, spouses set boundaries, but they were also willing to cross those boundaries if the need arose. Couples that have positive caregiving experiences use extended networks of family members, friends, or community organizations and services to help with the caregiving.

3. *Successful couple caregivers* try to prevent conflict and reduce stress during the caregiving experience.

The attitudes needed to prevent conflict and reduce stress include patience, sensitivity, tact, cooperation, good communication skills, emotional awareness, equal treatment of biological and in-law parents, and positive relations with others. Common sense thinking and group problem solving along with mutual respect are the key in promoting better relationships within the caregiving system.

4. *Successful couple caregivers* develop personality characteristics that will help them be good caregivers.

The attitudes needed to develop these personality characteristics include acceptance, openness, autonomy, environmental mastery, a need for personal growth, a purpose in life, and self-acceptance. These personality characteristics will promote psychological well-being and life satisfaction.

5. *Successful couple caregivers* use many strategies and adaptations to cope with caregiving experiences.

Attitudes of openness, fairness, autonomy, promptness, flexibility and humor are needed to use or adapt to new strategies and develop coping skills. Caregivers need to accept caregiving as part of their own life cycle. They need to learn to solve problems on a daily basis. They need to foster autonomy or independence in their care recipients while maintaining autonomy in their own lives.

6. *Successful couple caregivers* use their religious or spiritual beliefs in all aspects of caregiving; although, these beliefs affect motivation and relationships to a greater degree.

The attitude most needed for this area of success is simply a strong religious faith or spiritual belief. Couples use spirituality to add meaning to their caregiving experience, to foster better family relationships, to provide equality in caregiving, to promote psychological well-being, and to improve their life-satisfaction.

7. *Successful couple caregivers* know how and when to use extended help for respite care and intensive care.

The attitudes needed for a successful networking experience are openness, acceptance, trust, cooperation, persistence, the ability to compromise, and the ability to repress feeling of guilt.

Results of a positive attitude

Successful couple caregivers think their caregiving experiences are positive because

- They feel good about what they have accomplished.
- They have set a good example for their children.
- They have been shown appreciation by the care recipients, their siblings, and community individuals.
- They have shared many fun activities with the care recipients and other family members.
- They have fulfilled their spiritual needs.
- They have gained inner strength and personal growth.
- They have grown in knowledge that will help them in their own aging.

Summation

The results of good attitudes about caregiving lead to an abundance of aesthetics and intangible rewards in life. You need to look at the big picture. If your goals are money and fame, you won't achieve them by caregiving. If you want an abundance of beautiful feelings, integrity, and peace of mind ~ do caregiving.

Chapter Chuckle

You know you are getting older when . . .
* You get winded playing chess.
* You join a health club and don't go.
* Your mind makes contracts your body cannot meet.

PART II

WHEN I AM OLD
By Jenny Joseph

When I am an old woman I shall wear purple
with a red hat that doesn't go, and doesn't suit me,
and I shall spend my pension
on brandy and summer gloves
and satin sandals,
and say we've no money for butter.

I shall sit down on the pavement when I am tired,
and gobble up samples in shops and press alarm bells,
and run my stick along the public railings,
and make up for the sobriety of my youth.
I shall go out in my slippers in the rain
and pick the flowers in other people's gardens,
and learn to spit.

You can wear terrible shirts and grow more fat,
and eat three pounds of sausage at a go,
or only bread and pickles for a week,
and hoard pens and pencils and beer mats
and things in boxes.

But now we must have clothes that keep us dry,
and pay our rent and not swear in the street,
and set a good example for the children.

We will have friends to dinner and read the papers.
But maybe I ought to practice a little now?
So people who know me
are not too shocked and surprised,
when suddenly I am old
and start to wear purple!

"Somebody had to do it, for the love of our parent,
we naturally would."

Chapter 3

Motivation

Chapter Goal: To help caregivers understand motivation for caregiving and promote the attitudes necessary for proper motivation which will lead to successful caregiving.

What a dumb question!

When first asked what motivated them or why they chose to do the caregiving, many of the couples' first reactions were some *looks* that said, *"What a dumb question that is!"* As the question was defined and discussed, I discovered that most couples felt that taking care of their elderly parents was a natural, expected duty of adult children ~ their communities expected such behavior from them.

One husband's answer was right on target. He said, "I wonder what people in town would have thought of us if we wouldn't of taken care of our parents. *'They didn't even go to help their dad or mother!'* I think it's kind of the way it is in small communities. You have to help them [elders] until you're not able to help them anymore." Adult children who would not help their frail parents would be the topic of much negative conversation in the local coffee shops.

At first many couples could not think of what motivated them; however, as the interviews progressed, terms such as responsibility, love, obligation, pay back, elders' expectations, and spiritual beliefs emerged as motivators. According to the literature on what motivates adult children to care for elderly parents, that I reviewed for my study, these six terms represent the same factors that motivate anyone to do caregiving.

Just the facts, Mame!

The following six factors motivate all adult children to do caregiving:

1. *Affection,* which relates to the amount of attachment and love adult children have for their elderly parents.

2. *Responsibility,* which concerns the duties adult children feel they need to perform when taking care of their elderly parents.

3. *Reciprocity,* which relates to the exchange of rewards between adult children and elderly parents (pay back).

4. *Expectations of elders,* which relates to the fact that the elders took care of their children and parents and in turn expect to be taken care of when they get old.

5. *Obligation,* which concerns expectations of appropriate behavior that society has toward elder care by adult children.

6. *Religion/spirituality,* which relates to the affect religion or spirituality has in helping adult children cope with the caregiving of elderly parents.

"We **love** her," and "We **loved** them," were short answers often given when couples were asked about why they helped. Other statements that eloquently expressed **affection** were: "For the **love** of our parents," and "I **loved** my parents and his parents." Although words and emotions that reflected **affection** were more often used by wives, all of the husbands agreed with their wives on this issue with nods and body language. It seemed to be more difficult for the husbands to verbally express their affection for the elderly parents.

"I don't know that it was a **responsibility.** It was just the idea that it [caregiving] needed to be done; you just did it." The idea of finding a reason for doing caregiving was insignificant for some respondents because the sense of **responsibility** and duty were so ingrained in their personalities that the reasons for caregiving did not have to be defined or labeled. Most couples did not distinguish between **responsibility** (more of a duty) and **obligation** (more of a behavior). The depth of **responsibility** felt by the couples was expressed in the following statements: "Sometimes you put off your work and do theirs and then do yours, when you have time." "The caregiving always came first; it was what we did."

"I guess she put up with me a lot of years, so I thought I'd try putting up with her." "We did things for her she used to do for us." "Parents take care of their children, and kids should take care of their parents." "We were close to them all our lives, and I know if we were in that situation [helpless], they would take care of us." These statements show a desire to **reciprocate** [pay back] for some of the love and care that had been given to the adult children by the elders at earlier times in life. One wife summed it up best: "Our parents took care of us as children, so it's just no more than right for us to look after them when they are not able to take care of themselves anymore."

"She made us **feel kind of guilty** by saying, *'I always took care of my dad,'*" "As the years went by, they [elders] just **kind of assumed** that they could depend on you." "They **took it for granted**, but I'm sure they appreciated it." These statements show that many of the elderly parents **expected** their adult children to take care of them in their old age. This came through **loud and clear** in many interviews.

"I think that everyone is kind of **obligated** to their mom and dad when the time comes." "It's our place to do it. I'm her son." "I feel I didn't have a choice for I was the one living closest to them, and I could see them every day easily and watch over them." "It was the right thing to do." These statements showed that **obligations** were promoted by affection and a sense of morality.

"Honor your mother and your father." "Do onto others as you would have them do onto you." "Our faith has always been our guide." "I would have felt very un-Christian turning my back on my parents, and I think my husband would have, too, just because that is the way we were brought up." These statements reflected the effect religious training and faith had on the caregivers. I noted that some of the couples may have thought that questions on **religion** as a motivator meant "Did your pastor or church motivate you?" rather than "Did your own inner religious beliefs or spirituality help motivate you?" One wife's answer to my question clarified the two different meanings the question had for the couples: "It wasn't any organized religion, we never called a minister for help in this process. It was more in our personal faith and our faith in each other." Religious factors were so important to the people I interviewed that I devoted Chapter 8 to this topic.

For some of the individuals in the interviews, the caregiving became an ego thing. "It was nice to know someone appreciated what you've done," was a sentiment expressed or implied by many couples. **Appreciation** shown by siblings, spouses, and the elders being cared for was very rewarding to these caregivers. Compliments from members of the community and church, and setting a good example for their own children give these caregivers a sense of pride.

An important factor that emerged from this study, which was not found in any of the literature I reviewed, was the **equal motivation** by both spouses. All of the couples felt that both spouses were equally motivated to do the caregiving. Most of the husbands felt their wives had done more caregiving than they had done; however, wives felt their husbands were equally involved. The wives appreciated the support given by the husbands as well as the tasks they performed. "Just to know they're there is a great help," showed the appreciation of one wife for her husband's support. I think that one of the reasons that these caregiving experiences were so positive was because both spouses wanted to do the caregiving.

Getting it directly from the horse's mouth.
      To get a better understanding of how couples were motivated, I've chosen some dialogue from the interviews that will paint a picture of what motivated these couples to do caregiving and continue to do caregiving over a long period of time. Narrative will be used to introduce, clarify, and explain some of the dialogue used. While reading this dialogue, you may reach some epiphanies of your own. Different perspectives can be achieved when reading this material depending on the reader's insight, background, and personal experience. Your own personal translation of these short dialogues will make this material more meaningful for you.
      Many couples, when asked what motivated them, lumped **affection, responsibility, obligation, reciprocity, proximity**, or **life cycle process** together in their replies.
      A common response made by a farmer and echoed by many couples was, "Well, they are my parents and I am the one living right here. You just did it because they are your parents. You wanted to look after them." His wife added, "I'd agree. It was just kind of a **natural life process**." The husband went on to explain, "If one of my brothers would of lived here they would of done the same thing. I see them [parents] every day."
      The wife went on to explain how they got into the caregiving. "Also, it's a gradual thing. The transition from two independent families living here [on the farm]. They [elders] occasionally asked for help, here and there, and as the years went by it just gradually changed ~ we gave more and more help."
      The husband added, "You get started doing this caregiving and you don't even know you are doing it. We couldn't remember what day we started helping Mom and Dad because it's been going on for as long as

we've lived here, probably, but we didn't know it. Especially when you look at the question about emotional and social support. We've been doing that for 30 years or more. We didn't realize we were actually helping them."

Another couple's answers to motivation questions showed a need to **reciprocate.** The wife answered first: "When I took care of my mom she was living by herself. I just helped her out. I guess." Her husband continued, "Well, to put it point blank, she was too good to be in a nursing home and too bad to be alone. She had to have a place to stay."

I then asked the husband, "So you were kind of paying her back?"

"Trying, just trying. . . . I guess we never gave it a thought. You didn't say, *'I got to do this or I got to do that,'* you just did it."

Affection, responsibility and proximity were mentioned by one wife when she was asked about motivation. "We loved them. They needed help, and I was close." Her husband also suggested **reciprocity** as a reason. "Well, they took care of us when we needed help, when they needed help we were there for them ~ we lived close by." When this couple was asked what kept them motivated, they didn't think that keeping motivated was a problem. The husband's reply was slow and thoughtful. "Well, it's sometimes very discouraging but it's something you get over very fast. I don't think it's [keeping motivated] really a big problem." His wife was quicker with her answer. "It's not a problem to keep motivated. You just do it!"

The **expectations** of their elderly father were discussed at length by another couple. The wife explained, "Well, after helping with caregiving for my mother-in-law ~ she passed away and father was alone ~ it was our intention to move into town anyway, either into an apartment or into father's home. He [father] said, *'by all means.'* At first he didn't require much help. In fact, the first year he went away a couple months, but he didn't want to be alone in this big house."

I asked if the father **expected** his children to take care of him. The wife laughed. "Yes!" The husband also laughed and said, "Pretty well." The wife went on to explain, "When we cared for my mother-in-law, she should have been in a home because the last year she was incontinent, and it was difficult. We lived on the farm, but there were three of us siblings to take care of her then. He [father] said to my husband, *'She took care of you when you were a baby and you'll do it for her now!'* He wouldn't even hear of putting her into a home."

A working couple was asked if they thought their mother **expected** help. The husband replied, "Not anymore than any person. I'm only 65, but I figure that some day the time will come, when I need some help. We never talked about it that much. It was just something you think about and if they need some help ~ you are **obligated** to help them . . . ." His wife interrupted, "I think Mother was a very strong person. Very independent." The husband continued, "She [mother] kept on saying over and over, *'I don't want to be a burden to you. I don't want to bother you.'* She was really afraid that she'd take me away from my work. So coupled with that ~ she's almost furiously independent ~ she never really wanted to hinder us in our life. Lots of times we had to pry into her life to see if she needed something."

Many couples mentioned that even if their parents expected help, these **parents appreciated** the help they were given.

"Did your parents expect help?" I asked one of the younger couples. "Yes, I think so. I think they did," the husband replied with a laugh. His wife jumped into the conversation. "They appreciated it though." The husband agreed. "You bet." The wife explained, "They were fun to take care of because whatever you did was good. They never said, *'Oh you should of done it this way, or you should of done it that way.'* They would always say, *'Do it the way you want to do it and that's fine.'* They appreciated it."

Caregiving seemed to be a tradition in many families. Many of the couples I interviewed had parents and grandparent that had done caregiving for elders in the past. It was a way of life for them. Most of the couples were determined to see that this tradition would be passed on to the next generation. They also expected to be taken care of in their old, old age.

Summation

Proper motivation is essential for successful caregiving. The attitudes of appreciation, pride, self-esteem, integrity, and patience need to be developed. An understanding of human nature, a sense of belonging, a sense of accomplishment, a sense of importance, and a strong religious/ spiritual faith also help promote positive motivation.

Chapter Chuckle

You know you are getting older when . . .
* Your children begin to look middle-aged.
* You know all the answers, but nobody asks you the questions.
* The gleam in your eye is the sun hitting your bifocals.

"You do what you have to do whether it's your folks or a neighbor. Everybody needs help. If you're able to give it to them ~ you do."

Chapter 4

Role and Tasks

Chapter goal: To help caregivers understand the roles they will play and the attitudes necessary to accomplish tasks that lead to successful caregiving.

Knowing, doing, understanding
Knowing what types of work a caregiver would have to do, doing what comes naturally, understanding why Mom only wants her daughter's help, knowing how to set boundaries, knowing who can be counted on to help, understanding how the level of care goes from bad to worse, understanding the sacrifices you'll need to make at your own job, and swallowing your pride to ask for outside help are all important areas of caregiving to look into before you jump into the water.

The following comments were made when I asked couples about the roles they played or the tasks they performed during their caregiving years.

- "I think it was a little challenging at times to take care of her. That may be what made it interesting, just to see what was going to happen next."
- "Simple things are easy. When they become incontinent, it gets very hard."
- "I think the things I did for my mother were just about exactly what she did for her mother-in-law."
- "Like I mentioned earlier ~ helping my mother bathe ~ she was more comfortable having me do it."
- "She [wife] did what she did best and I [husband] did what I did best. That way we didn't argue about it."
- "We got lots of emotional support from our families ~ even the one's that aren't here."
- "It sure helped to know there was someone else you could talk to."

- "A person with Alzheimer's couldn't be by themselves. It's definitely helpful when they got their mind. They can give you credit for what you are doing and that makes you want to do more. If there is no feedback ~ I don't know ~ that would be a minus ~ I would say."
- "Dad and Mother were in a mobile home when I first started helping [caring for a dying mother]. I went up to relieve Dad at first because everyone else in the family was working."
- "Outside services were very helpful. Without them we couldn't have done it [caregiving]. The county nurse came; she was very good."
- "I don't think it's [caregiving] for anybody to tackle unless they have extra help. One person couldn't do it alone."

What, why, how, and when

To develop a **positive attitude** about the roles you will play and the tasks you will do during the caregiving experience requires a knowledge and understanding of those roles and tasks while caregiving. Eight themes and issues that emerged from the interviews are important to understand before going into the caregiving experience:

1. *What types of tasks will be performed?* Are the tasks ADLs or IADLs? ADL tasks like helping elders to eat, bathe, or walk, are most often performed by women; however, in some cases, men will do these tasks. The primary caregiver needs to know who is willing to help with ADL tasks because if no other family member will help with these tasks, that primary caregiver will be totally responsible for the most demanding caregiving. IADL task can be performed by almost anyone in the family or network of helpers that are available through churches and community-based organizations.

2. *Why are traditional and non-traditional roles important?* Traditional roles are performed by a specific gender according to the customs of a society. Doing traditional work (women cooking, men shoveling snow) proved successful for the couples interviewed because each spouse knew what they had to do and was competent at doing those tasks. Some couples did non-traditional work. This also worked well if the ground rules were set ahead of time and both spouses knew what was expected. Good communication that defines roles is essential before the caregiving begins.

3. *Why is gender preference by elders important?* Most elders prefer same gender care for personal needs and sometimes for other needs. Most of the elders now being cared for were raised in a time when modesty was a norm. They do not want to be undressed or bathed by strangers or members of their opposite sex. Future elders may have different attitudes. It is important for caregivers of a mother, for example, to understand that the female spouse may have to do most of the ADL care.

4. *How does defining roles and tasks promote job clarification?* Communication is the key word for promoting job clarification. Caregivers must know their family roles, what tasks they need to do, and be competent in doing these tasks. Brainstorming, setting boundaries, open discussions, and fairness are needed to prevent conflict, bitterness, and self-pity.

5. *What extended network help is available?* There is usually help available from children, siblings, and community members; in most cases, all you have to do is ask. To enter the caregiving experience without some reliable extended network of helpers is folly. Caregiving can last for ten or more years. To be a primary caregiver without any help can take its toll on the caregivers' mental and physical health.

6. *How does the care level affect caregiving?* The more care an elder needs the more skilled the caregiver must be. Know your abilities and limits. Not everyone is a competent nurse. When the care gets to the point were nursing skills are needed, outside help may be sought to assist the primary caregiver.

7. *How does work involvement and flexibility at work affect caregiving?* The more involved in work (other than caregiving) a caregiver is, the less flexibility they have to do caregiving ~ another no-brainer. Don't even think about taking on the job of a primary caregiver if you have a demanding job and a family to care for ~ it can't be done! Something will crack and it will probably be you. If you decide to do caregiving, create flexibility in your job and other family life. You must make time for the elder you care for ~ that includes social time ~ or you will be dealing with a very unhappy elder, who can make your life miserable.

8. *When should caregivers use outside services?* Public services such as the county nurse, Meals on Wheels, home health care, and government paid financial consultants are available in most places. When

the tasks become beyond your ability, you must have the wisdom to seek outside help.

Going to the source

Now that you know what constitutes the area of roles and tasks during caregiving, lets look at some dialogues which highlight some of the eight points discussed earlier in this chapter.

Most, but not all, of the couples did **traditional tasks.** I asked a husband whose wife worked full-time during their caregiving years, "Did you do any cooking?" He replied, "I can, but I'm not a very good cook. I can take care of myself, but I would not be a very good cook for anyone else." His wife added, "Lots of times he cooked. Especially when my parents required medical attention. I'd take my dad to Bismarck for three or four days at a time and he'd have to fend for himself. He survived pretty well."

Another couple was asked if they thought of tasks as "men's work or women's work?" The wife replied, "I guess I just did what I though I could. Some things are pretty simple, like a screw is out ~ I could do that. But if it was something I couldn't do, I'd have to call him [husband]." I asked this couple if they were socialized to do the roles and tasks they did. The husband replied, "I can remember as a kid going up to Grandma's and mowing the lawn, fixing the well, and things like that, when those chores needed to be done. Basically, I do the same things now. It's just part of a job that has to be done."

One couple, who was **very traditional** in their work roles and tasks, was asked the reason for this. The husband replied, "I don't know. She went ahead and did that [inside work] and I went ahead and did other things [outside work]." The wife added, "I was in the house and around to do what I did. He was out in the fields and not around so much. He's not used to that kind of thing anyway [giving medicine, cooking, cleaning, etc.]." That last statement brought a big laugh from both the spouses. I got the feeling that this couple though some work was women's and some was men's, accepted the way things were done, and liked it that way.

Not all of the spouses did **traditional work.** A husband who cooked meals for his elderly father was asked why he did this. "I cooked meals the last three weeks he was at home before he went into the nursing home. I stayed with him day and night. That's why I did all the meals." I asked him if he was a good cook. His wife said, "Yes he is." The husband then went on to explain that his dad was a good cook and did much of the family cooking because his mother had worked outside the home. The son learned to cook by watching his dad model cooking. This son had been a bachelor for many years and had to take care of himself.

Another husband who did many **non-traditional** tasks put it this way: "I guess when I was young we [mother and son] made cakes together and everything. We milked cows on the farm and every night after supper, with just the two boys, we had to wash the dishes and help with everything else." The mother of this son had socialized him to do non-traditional work, and he thought nothing of helping out with the housework. **Parents take note:** if you want your son's to help take care of you when you get old, teach them how to do housework when they are young.

A good example of **gender preference** occurred when I asked a daughter-in-law why she did most of the personal caregiving for her mother-in-law. She replied, "I think it's a lady's job to do for a lady. Often Mother would say, *'Don't send my son.'* It was her wish and I felt it was my duty ~ it was up to me." This woman's husband also stated that he felt household duties should be done by his wife because these were tasks she'd done *naturally* all her life.

In another family where the son was the primary caregiver for his elderly father, **gender preference** was present. The son did most of the personal care for his father. I asked if the elder had a gender preference and the wife replied, "He's more comfortable having his son do it [personal caregiving]. My husband is good at this, too. He often does these things [nursing type functions]." I then noted that the siblings in the family were all males, which might make a difference in their attitude toward personal hygiene caregiving because there were no sisters to do the work. The wife replied, "I can see that." The husband humbly added, "It's just a service I do."

A daughter gave a good example of her mother's **caregiving preference.** "We had a home health aid, but Mother is an extremely modest person, which is a reflection of the time period in which she was brought up, so it was more comfortable for her to have me bathe her." This wife also mentioned that all the elders she took care of preferred her cooking to others [including her husband's] because, "I learned to cook from my mother and mother-in-law, so they were all more comfortable with my home cooking than pizza."

Although most elders preferred the same gender to help them with personal hygiene tasks, some would let the opposite gender do some of these tasks if the preferred gender was not present. Spouses only crossed the gender line when doing personal hygiene tasks if there were no other alternatives.

Most couples set **boundaries** when it came to performing tasks and defining roles. A majority of spouses were the primary caregivers of their own parents while the in-law spouse was a secondary caregiver, except in several cases where daughter-in-laws were primary caregivers to in-laws. In these cases the son approved of the work arrangement but made the final decisions concerning his parent(s). When these boundaries were established, there was no question as to who would make the final decisions for their own parents. "She takes care of her parents and I take care of mine," was a statement made by one husband. His wife nodded a yes, and looked like she was in total agreement with him.

All of the couples had an **extended network** of helpers. Children were one source of help. "Our kids were extremely close to both sets of grandparents. My parents were able to attend all the kid's school functions, so the kids knew them pretty well. The kids liked to help them [elders] when they got older. They [children] were really good about picking up grandma's groceries and taking them to her place. The kids helped with mowing lawns and other chores, too." This type of dialogue was repeated in one form or another throughout a majority of the interviews.

Another wife explained how her **children helped**: "Our oldest son helped, but the other two didn't because they live far away. When they come home, they help with whatever they can do. Our oldest son was there everyday ~ twice a day for about four years." Her husband added, "That's about it I suppose. He'd [oldest son] get her [elder] up and get her going in the morning and then the home health care nurse would come and bathe her and things like that." The wife concluded, "Then he'd check her house and lock it up at night."

Help from siblings was also given. A son who lived with his elderly father explained how the family worked together to take care of the frail elder. "I was retired at the time [during the intensive caregiving] so I had some time to help. Both of us [husband and wife] were here with him [elder]. My brother, he's twenty years younger than me, was here, too." The wife agreed. "Yeah, he [brother] has a steady job . . . but he helped a lot. When we went somewhere, even for a Sunday afternoon, I'd give his brother a ring and he'd come over and check on Dad."

A wife told of how all the **siblings** in her husband's family had worked together to do an intervention to get the parents into a basic-care nursing facility. The husband added, "The three of us went to their house and they [elders] could see something was up." His wife continued, "The three really supported each other because it was hard for all three of them." The husband concluded, "My siblings had no qualms about putting Mom and Dad into basic care. They were very understanding."

A couple who had stated that their **son helped** take care of an elderly mother at times also discussed help they had gotten from church friends. The husband started the conversation: "People from the church have been very helpful. When we're gone on a vacation or go to see our kids, they help. There have been times when they have gone over to Mother's apartment and checked in on her." His wife jumped into the conversation: "Before she was in the nursing home." The husband continued: "Before she was in a nursing home, they'd pay a call on her just to see how she was and if there was anything she needed. A couple of ladies from the church took her shopping or took her for rides. Mother lived in a place where there were many older ladies, and they all kind of took care of each other."

Another daughter told about the help her dad's **friend** had given. "With my dad he had a really good friend who would help him with numerous things, and then they would play cribbage. I had an aunt and uncle, Dad's sister, who would come ~ maybe twice a year ~ and the uncle would help with yard work; that was his forte. They also gave emotional and social support and would go different places with Dad, when he was still able to go." The husband joined in, "The aunt and uncle stayed maybe three weeks. He [the uncle] would fix lots of things."

I then asked the husband if they had an **extended network** of caregivers. He replied with enthusiasm, "Oh definitely. With all the support from us and all those others, there isn't either one of them [elderly fathers] that couldn't of been living by themselves." (He thought I'd asked if the elder had an extended network of help.)

His wife continued, "My husband's dad also had a sister that would come and help him." The husband added, "Oh, yeah." The wife continued, "She did lots of things for him." The husband added, "She helped a lot but she had lots of time, too." (The sister was retired.) The wife concluded, "So what he [father] couldn't do, she would sometimes do." All of the couples had extended help networks. They used these networks sparingly. All of the couples appreciated any help they got from their care networks, especially if that help was volunteered and willingly given.

Alzheimer's disease was a big topic of discussion when it came to the **level of care needed**. This disorder seemed to be the most devastating because the elders were sometimes physically fit, but their mental capacities were limited.

One couple talked about three of their parents' physical and mental conditions. The husband started the discussion: "My mother was fairly healthy until she went into the hospital with terminal cancer and passed away. There were a few financial things, but she was mostly on her own." The wife continued: "My husband's mother was mentally capable until she died." Her husband added, "It wasn't as much of a problem as her parents because her mom has Alzheimer's disease, and her dad is in a wheelchair now. So, it's a little different situation." The wife added sadly, "Yes, my parents are living longer." (The wife was suggesting that the longer people live the more intensive care they need).

Work and flexibility in work and lifestyle were issues often discussed. Most of the couples had one or both spouses that had flexibility in their daily work or jobs. These couples explained their flexibility in many ways as the following dialogues demonstrate.

A couple where both spouses worked full-time had **different shifts** to work, so the caregiving they did with their father worked out okay. The husband stated, "I worked days, and I'd be home with him at night. She worked some nights and some days." His wife added, "He [husband] didn't mind me working nights because it was nice to have his dad here."

Another couple explained how they made **flexibility** in their jobs by working **different shifts**, going to **part-time work**, using **sibling help**, and also taking **early retirement**. The husband explained, "I was working when caregiving first started, but by the time he got really sick I was pretty much done with work. I sometimes would haul hay. When I was busy with that, my sister came and helped. She stayed and helped Dad while we did our chores."

The wife next explained her job situation. "My job started at 3:00 p.m. and ended sometime late at night. I never had to go to my parent's home during that time. I did the caregiving in the morning. That wasn't a problem until toward the end. I finally decided I couldn't do it all, so I quit my job. That was toward the end when they [elders] were really sick. I took early retirement."

I asked a farm couple, "Since you are a farmer and your wife does not work outside the home, do you have a lot of **work flexibility**?" The husband quickly answered, "Right." His wife agreed to the statement I had made. Self-employed farmers whose spouses didn't work off the farm had the most flexibility in their work schedules.

The use of **outside services** was a two-edged sword. Some people liked outside help, and others did not. All agreed that there were times you had no other choice.

A positive look at outside services

Question: "Did you use any professional services or outside services?"

Wife: "Yes, there was a time when my dad had bypass surgery and the nurses from Carrington came to help. They would come every day to take care of his dressings and make him do his exercises."

Question: "Was that the only time you used professional services?"

Wife: "The county nurse came the first Monday of every month and we'd always make sure my folks went up to see her. Then she checked them out, talked to them, and explained things to them. The county nurse was the one that convinced my mother she should go into the nursing home after my dad was put into the home. She reinforced what the family was planning to do."

Question: "She was helpful?"

Wife: "She was very helpful. The doctors and nurses were excellent, but they weren't here every day."

Question: "Did these doctors and nurses give you any advice on how to do caregiving?"

Wife: "Oh, yes!"

Question: [to husband] "How about you?"

Husband: "The only help my dad had was the county nurse. He used to go up there and have his blood pressure checked. Nobody came to his house."

Question: [to wife] "Your folks got Meals on Wheels, but your husband's dad did not?"

Wife: "They went up to the Senior Citizen's Center about three times a week for meals, and also they got to see people regularly. People would also go there to visit."

Husband: "They did bring my dad meals, but other than that he wouldn't go up to the senior center, if he never got a bite to eat."

Wife: "His dad wasn't that type."

Husband: "No, he wasn't the type to mix."

Wife: "Yes, and another service that was extremely helpful is a lady who comes once a month and takes care of insurance . . . and helps with paying the doctor bills. She is so helpful in many ways. She works for South Central Adult Services."

Husband: "All the stuff comes back from Medicare, and you don't know what it is; she helps."

Wife: "It's a bigger regional thing, but she's the representative for this area. People need to know about this service. It's just tremendous what she does. I would have been lost and disheartened if I had to take care of all the medical bills and understand what they were saying, but all I had to do was call her and she'd say, *'Lets go over this,'* and I'd write out the checks. She's gotten some of the secondary insurances to come across with more money than they would have otherwise. She calls them up, and they pay more."

A negative look at outside services

Question: "Did you ever use any outside services?"

Wife: "I think I had a home health aid one time for my mother to help her take a bath. Mother wouldn't have her after that."

Husband: "My dad wouldn't take Meals on Wheels."

Wife: "Neither would my mother."

Question: "Did you get any advice from professionals like doctors and nurses?"

Wife: "No, because they don't know anything about caregiving. You can't give advice if you've never walked the walk. They can tell you physically what is happening to them [elders], you already know that because you can see that."

Question: "So maybe what you're saying is that there might be a need for our doctors and nurses in the health profession to brush up on elder caregiving?"

Wife: "They aren't going to do it unless there is a stipend involved."

Husband: "Well, the doctor did tell my dad he couldn't go home after his surgery because he couldn't take care of himself ~ that didn't stop him!"

Wife: "That was obvious!" [elder couldn't take care of himself]

Husband: "He fell down and couldn't get up. That's when he decided he couldn't be at home anymore. They [doctors and nurses] don't spend much time with the elderly."

Question: "Don't doctors go into the nursing homes and check elders once in a while?"

Wife: "Once a month or two months or three months. They usually send a P.A."

Question: "Oh, so it's not a lengthy visit? It's just 'hello, how are you, good-bye.'"

Wife: "Exactly!"

Most of the couples did not use outside help except the voluntary services of close relatives, if they could do the caregiving tasks required. Help was used very sparingly for respite care and tasks that required professional training. Nursing homes were used extensively when caregiving became very intensive and time consuming. Nursing home care will be discussed in Chapter 9.

Summation

Effective roles and efficient task completion are essential when taking on the job of caregiving for an elderly parent. Empathy, cooperation, a good work ethic, understanding others' feelings, the ability to change, and the ability to sacrifice are attitudes that need to be achieved to accomplish the roles and tasks that are necessary for successful caregiving.

Chapter Chuckle

You know you are getting old when . . .

- You look forward to a dull evening.
- Your favorite part of the newspaper is "Twenty-five Years Ago Today."
- Your romantic conversations with your spouse consist of one word ~ **"What?"**

"There was nothing, really, it just seemed to work out all right. I think something like this is just common sense. Something that has to be done is just done. I don't think anyone ever questioned a decision made. There was no problem."

Chapter 5

Family Relationships

Chapter Goal: To help caregivers prevent conflict and reduce stress by understanding the attitudes necessary to accomplish these two important aspects for successful caregiving.

What conflict ~ stress ~ burden?

Talking about relationships that took place during the caregiving was a difficult topic for many of the couples to discuss. The three broad areas covered in this category were **conflict, stress,** and **burden.** When asked if there was any conflict in relationships during the caregiving experience, a majority of the couples immediately answered "no." As the topic was pursued, all of the couples admitted to some **conflict, stress,** or **burden** ensued during the caregiving.

None of the couples mentioned **conflict** in their marriages. "Life is too short to fight" was a comment made by one wife. Since the spouses were interviewed together, they may not have wanted to get into any marital conflict discussions in front of their spouse. I observed during the interviews that the spouses were very compatible. They took turns talking, they asked each other's opinions, they looked at each other for confirmation of answers, they agreed to almost everything said by their partner, and they showed respect for each other's opinion. I believe that caregiving did not cause conflict in these couples' marriages, and in some cases the marriages may have been strengthened by the experience.

Another factor, in my opinion, that helped reduce conflict was the attitude both spouses had toward their in-laws. All individuals talked about both sets of parents as Mother/Mom and Father/Dad. I could tell from their tone of voice and body language, that it didn't make any difference if they were taking care of a biological parent or an in-law parent ~ their attitudes about the caregiving were always positive.

All of the couples discussed situations where there was **stress** in the caregiving. One husband summed this up very thoughtfully when he stated, "If you care enough, it will cause some stress. If you don't care enough to cause stress, you would have no feelings at all toward them [elders]." Since getting old can be a difficult process, I would have to agree with this husband's statement.

Some causes of **stress** mentioned by the couples were:

- Negative attitudes of siblings
- Elders' needs to be independent
- Negative attitudes of elders
- Demands of elders
- Lack of appreciation by elders
- Unnecessary household duties performed for elders
- Personality clashes between elders and adult children
- Unhappiness with nursing homes expressed by elders
- Crowded schedules of adult children
- Job conflicts
- Decision making
- Role reversal

"All in all it was very stressful, but it was part of the life process" was a summation of the caregiving experience by one wife. This conclusion was expressed in one form or another by most of the couples. These couples all had **some stress**, but they did not dwell on it because they accepted the stress as part of their life cycle. "It had to be done . . . so you just did it" was the sentiment echoed by many caregivers, especially husbands. A positive attitude toward the caregiving went a long way to prevent or reduce stress for these couples.

Burden was rarely mentioned and never elaborated on by any of the couples because they all had gone into the caregiving voluntarily; therefore, they did not consider caregiving a burden. One wife commented after her mother-in-law had been put into the nursing home, "It was a burden lifted, when she went into the home."

When asked about **conflict,** one husband replied, "There really wasn't any. At times you felt you were **burdened**, or you felt you really couldn't do this . . . you kept doing what you were doing till you couldn't do it any longer." A wife who worked a full-time job didn't think caregiving was much of a problem: "Oh, you **get stressed** occasionally, I guess. You'd get kind of stressed because you'd have to do so many things, and you'd be tired when you came home from work. You still had to go check on Gramps. If he hadn't eaten anything ~ if I had fixed a meal here ~ I'd take something to him. Like I said before, it was just occasionally. You just worked it out." One couple who had taken care of all four elderly parents over a long period of time mentioned the word **burden** only once, when the wife talked about caring for a dying father-in-law for two months in their home.

Positive attitudes of resolve and commitment helped prevent conflict and reduced stress for these couples. One individual summed it up best: "You're bound to have a bad day, when you become frustrated and feel tapped ~ that's part of caregiving ~ nothing in your life is going to be perfect."

In your face!

Read the following dialogues by the fifteen couples interviewed and decide for yourself how much conflict, stress, or burden these people experienced during their caregiving years.

When asked about **conflict,** a farmer's wife told this story: "I remember once, when I went to her house, I didn't mind doing things for my mother-in-law, but she had tons of plants. They were beautiful plants, but one day I just got mad. She said, *'We've got to put miracle-grow on those plants today.'* I said, *'I don't know why you have to have all these plants.'* She said, *'Well, that's what I like.'* Then I said, *'If you can't take care of them, you should get rid of them.'"* [Everyone laughed] "She had all these things she wanted to keep just like when she took care of her own things; that's the only time I can ever remember that I really got upset. It was more work for me."

I questioned the wife, "Did she get rid of the plants?" The wife replied, "Oh, no." [Everyone laughed] "I continued watering them whether they needed it or not." Then she continued her story about the mother-in-law's dog. "Taking care of her was easy ~ that dog! I hated that dog. It was awful, but we put up with him. . . ." Both of these stories were told with tenderness and laughter. Both spouses laughed all the way through the stories.

Another couple was asked if there was any **conflict** in the family during the caregiving that had to be resolved. The wife looked at her husband before she answered, "I don't remember any." Her husband agreed, "Not that I know of anyway." The wife continued, "Our sister in California didn't think the folks should have moved out of their house and sold the house." Her husband added, "Yes, but your mother handled that." The wife agreed, "Yes. Dad was dead. Mother got an opportunity to sell the house and she did. My other sister and I helped Mother find an apartment after the house was sold." I questioned, "It sounds like your mother was making her own decisions?" The wife replied, "Very much so." I summed up the discussion: "So even if your out-of-state sister didn't like the decision, she had to respect your mother's decision?" The wife answered smiling, "Yes."

It was much easier to deal with siblings who lived long distances from their frail elders, when the parents could help with the decision making. This came through loud and clear in most of the conversations about uncooperative siblings.

Another wife told of a fussy father: "For the most part, I'd say our fathers were very easy to get along with. They were **appreciative** for whatever you would do for them. They weren't very demanding. Early on, my dad was kind of funny. He had a certain way of doing things. He was a good cook and you had to peel the tomatoes just right. If you didn't do it that way, he'd get frustrated. So I said, *'I'll try and do it your way, Dad.* [Laughs] *I don't know if I can do it as good as you.'* That type of thing ~ just small things."

An example of **conflict** came to light when a couple with a very determined mother had several stories to tell about their relationship with her:

Wife: "If you said, 'No, we can't do this today,' she'd say, *'Why can't we?'* She always wanted to go to Jamestown. I took her to Jamestown sometimes three times a week. If I would tell her 'no,' she'd argue till she got her way."

Question: "Did you try to explain your reasons for saying no?"

Wife: "She wouldn't listen to reason."

Husband: "She wouldn't hear you."

Wife: "Then she'd come back and say, *'Then I'll get somebody else to take me.'* She would make us feel guilty. You better do it because she wants to do it. The sad part about it was that it was not important that we go. She got it into her head that she was going and that was that."

Question: "Did you usually give in?"

Wife: "I usually gave in."

Question: "Just to please her?"

Wife: "I spoiled her at first and in the later years we paid for it because we'd always done it her way. She was a determined lady. Sometimes we'd talk to her and try to work it out."

Husband: "Well, sometimes when she wanted to go to Jamestown, she wouldn't tell us why, so I'd say, *'is this a wild goose chase or is it something you really have to go for?'* [Laughs] She knew what I meant because she just wanted to be out; she didn't have anything to go for."

Question: "Could you tease her or humor her into seeing your point of view?"

Husband: "I don't know if we humored her or not. [Laughs] Sometimes if we were busy she'd understand. She really didn't have any reason to go. If the weather was bad, or you'd tell her it was going to snow, she'd say, *'Well, I'm not going to go then.'* We didn't lie to her about it but she wouldn't go if the weather was bad."

Question: "So you could reason with her at times? You probably tried to humor her a little?"

Husband: "Yes."

The husband in this last couple was better at dealing with his mother than his wife was. The wife later explained that she had a more difficult time dealing with the mother-in-law because their **personalities were so different**. The mother was very conservative, messy, and liked to be in control. The wife was less conservative, very neat, and subservient. I also noticed, with this couple and several others, that some spouses spoiled their parent(s) at the beginning of the caregiving and later paid for that lack of discipline. Dealing with elders is similar to dealing with young children. You need to be firm, fair, and in control or they tend to take advantage of you. The spouse that was the best disciplinarian usually got along better with the elder and had less stress in their lives.

Another couple quickly answered no to **family conflicts** when they were asked, but later admitted they had some sisters that were disagreeable:

Question: "Were there any conflicts that you can think of?"

Husband: "No, I don't think so."

Wife: "There may have been if you would of had to spend a lot of time in the caregiving, days, hours . . ."

Question: [to the husband] "You did mention earlier that your sisters didn't show up a whole lot? Did that ever make you mad?"

Wife: "No, not at all; we let it be."

Husband: "Yeah, just let it be."

Wife: "There was nothing you could do about it."

Husband: "My dad used to go see my sister, and we took him out there to see her a couple times."

Wife: "Then too, she worked a lot of those years, so he didn't want to stay long."

Husband: "He got so he didn't want to make the long trip anymore."

Wife: "It wasn't the fact that they [sisters] didn't come very often, it was how they acted when they came. That was the problem."

Question: "Can you expand on that a bit?"

Wife: "They were just ~ I don't know what the trouble was. They felt they were getting cheated or something. They wanted to control our father and he wasn't going to be controlled. That was the bottom line."

A retired couple talked about **conflict** in their caregiving experience:

Wife: "I was more into the caregiving than my husband. I planned our schedule around the things my father-in-law wanted to do. Maybe that was part of the problem here?"

Question: "What do you mean by that?"

Wife: "Father got more attention from me than my husband did lots of times."

Question: "Oh, I see."

Wife: "Does that make sense?"

Question: "You may be right about that. Tell me more?"

Wife: "It's not that once in a while I didn't get impatient with Father, it's just that I would walk away from it. My husband used to lose his temper once in a while. Father couldn't hear him anyway. [The father had a hearing problem] Like I said, my husband thought his father was supposed to be the father he always was. [Role reversal] It was hard for my husband to accept the things his Father said and did. Father became a *know it all* and things like that would bother my husband. This got worse as senility set in; that's not the way he [elder] used to be."

Question: [to the husband] "How do you feel about that?"

Husband: "Oh I don't know . . . I got along with him when we did yard work. I didn't listen to him. I just went out ~ cut a few trees down ~ even if he didn't want us to. He didn't like it. I didn't like it either when I wanted to look out the window and couldn't see the street because of the trees, so we cut them down. He wasn't too happy with that. Dad was a hard worker. He did everything by hand. He hayed with horses. He never had a loader. When he quit the farming and moved to town, the first thing I did was buy a farm hand hay loader."

Wife: "When we planted the garden, he [father] would sit in a lawn chair and say, *'Do this ~ put this in there,'* so I'd do it my way even if he was still watching. I had planted garden for 35 years and knew how to do it. [Laughs] I would just smile at him and he'd say, *'Oh, you're doing it that way?'* I'd just go ahead and do it."

Question: "So you more or less handled conflict by doing what you wanted?"

Both spouses laughed at this question. The husband concluded, "I took care of it." Later in the interview I commented that the personalities of the father and the husband seemed to be similar. Both spouses agreed to that statement and felt the similarity in personalities may have contributed to the conflict between the father and son. Both father and son liked to be in control.

One son experienced stress when his mother put his father into a nursing home. The father blamed the son for putting him into the home.

Husband: "From the day he went into the home until he passed away, he never talked to me."

Wife: "We're sure that Dad thought we put him into the home."

Husband: "I think that he [father] thought I was the one that put him there. I didn't have anything to do with it."

Question: "Did the doctor recommend it?"

Wife: "Yes."

Husband: "Well, they did to my mother. I didn't argue with her. I didn't want to see him go into the home but she couldn't handle him and we couldn't go to their place to take care of him all the time. We had our own jobs and were very busy . . . in fact, if he'd stayed in that apartment he would of fallen and hurt himself and maybe her too. So, he had to go into the home. It's just one of those things in life. There are a lot of things you don't want to do, but you have to do them. It had to be done and I still think he thought I was the one that did it. I guess it's better that he blamed me than my mother."

Wife: "He [father] would of taken it out on her."

Husband: "Yeah."

Wife: "He could get dissatisfied with her ~ ugly with her."

Husband: "He got that way once in a while, but I don't think he knew it."

This son felt very badly about the relationship he and his father had the last few months of the father's life. The son suffered the consequences of his dad's silence to protect his mother from possible verbal abuse.

Another wife admitted that she was often frustrated because her mother-in-law never **appreciated** anything she did. "I did my best. My best was not good enough often times."

A **stressful situation** for a farmer's wife was to have to make all the **decisions** connected with the caregiving. "I guess one of the hardest things about doing caregiving is ~ there are six of us siblings ~ when our parents got very sick and needed extra care, deciding how much more care and doctoring you're going to do. It was stressful making all the decisions. *'Was it going to be all right with the rest of the family?'* I shouldn't have let it bother me because if they wanted ~ some of them were retired ~ they could of done it themselves, if they weren't satisfied. Toward the end, they came home quite often, and they never did say anything ~ that I wasn't doing things right."

I asked her, "Did you ever **brainstorm** with your siblings? Call them and tell them about what was happening and asked what you should do?" She replied, "When my mother went into the nursing home, I called my sister because the ones away don't see what's going on, and they don't think the elders are as bad as they are. I said to my sister, *'We're putting Mother into the nursing home.'* I told her if she thought she could come home and take care of Mother the opportunity was hers ~ I knew I couldn't do it. She never said anything. She didn't want to do it. [Laughs] They [siblings] didn't really say much about anything like that, but I do know that they ~ the one's that aren't here ~ don't know how bad it is or what's going on. They think the old people don't have to be in the nursing home. When it gets to a certain point, the old people have to be in a nursing home ~ it's a good place for them."

Another wife's answer to the stress question involved **scheduling and work.** "There is always stress. You need a lot of patience ~ a lot of patience when working with elderly people. There were times when I just didn't want to go and take my mother shopping or to buy groceries, but you just did it. It was a little stressful when I had other things to do. My husband's father was even more difficult because he though he could do everything himself." Her husband joined the conversation: "Yes, but he had everything done the way he wanted to and nobody was going to change his mind. You couldn't find out much from him, he didn't tell you much, he just told you what he wanted you to know. He had everything pretty well arranged."

I reflected what this couple had said, "So, one stressful problem was that the caregiving probably interfered with your own schedules and what you wanted to do?" The wife answered first, "I think so. My mother was in the nursing home three years, so she got a little cantankerous occasionally. You just kind of had to put up with that. I probably would be the same way if I were in her place."

A second story about caregiving that interfered with work was told by a son. "There were times when in the past year ~ especially during springs work ~ when my parents had doctors' appointments. If I hadn't been in the field, I would have driven them, but they went and drove themselves. We didn't feel comfortable about it, but it was like *'what are we going to do?'* I couldn't stop seeding wheat every time they have a problem. We had a life, too." His wife added, "Your dad would say, *'Today I'm having a good day.'* It was like he was saying, *'Don't tell me I can't drive to town today.'"* The son concluded, "Yup, maybe he was telling us, *'You can't take us today so we are going to go ourselves.'"*

Role reversal was the most often mentioned **stressor**. A talkative wife went into much detail to explain how tough **role reversal** was. "I think it was the hardest, when talking about roles, when your parents get older and you take on the supervisory roles. You're more used to parents, even as you get older, being the supervisors. You have a lot of respect for your parents' opinions, then when it gets to where their opinions don't always make sense, and you have to take on the supervisory position and say, *'You can't drive anymore,'* that is the hardest thing to do. The driving thing was big. It's overwhelming when that happens. Now, you have to tell them what things they can't do anymore. It's an adjustment for them, too. . . . *'You have to take this medicine, Dad; you have to take it.'* That kind of stuff; it's almost like they become children again."

One couple told many humorous stories about their father's driving when he got old. **Role reversal** was a big problem because the father shouldn't have been driving, but he wouldn't listen to the adult children. The wife started the story: "Father drove a car a lot longer than he should have. He drove any which way ~ anyplace. He felt that as long as he had a disability sign hanging in his car he could do anything. He parked by fire hydrants. You had to laugh at the things that happened ~ maybe not in front of him. The police would come and tell us about his poor driving. We'd say, *'Go after him, he isn't going to listen to us.'*"

Her husband went on with the story: "I told the police, *'I can't do anything, you guys have to do something.'* For many years Father couldn't parallel park, so he'd drive up on the curve with the back end of the car sticking out."

His wife summed it up: "There were lots of things we used to laugh at. Our brother, who lives next door, would come over and say, *'You will never guess what Dad did today.'*"

A couple that spent a considerable amount of time talking about **role reversal** felt sorry for the elders because they were losing their **independence**. "One of the hardest things for me was doing my dad's business for him," the wife said thoughtfully. "When he was in the nursing home, he thought he could have all the money he wanted in his billfold, and he thought he should have his checkbook in there, too. So this was a very sore subject at first. I tried to explain to him that there are people who will take advantage of the elderly. I put money in his billfold once but he lost it. We had an awful time about him wanting his checkbook. I didn't give in too easily on that. I went to the bank and took out a checkbook account for only $500, so dishonest people couldn't get too much out of him. That stopped him from hounding me about it. I could see his point, too. When my parents got married, they didn't have anything. There wasn't anything to be had and it took lots of years ~ raising kids ~ to make a go of it until they did have something and then *'bingo'*, you can't have what you do have. [Everyone laughed] It's pretty tough when you take everything away from them. That's what they feel is happening, I think."

Her husband joined in, "When we look back, into their minds ~ and we will be no different ~ it's hard for them to lose the **independence** that they've had. They were just doing things like other people before going into the home, and then they have to rely on other people to do everything for them. That is hard for them to accept. To be truthful, *'I don't want them darned kids to tell me what to do.'* That's just it. Sure there are a lot of times you've got to just grit your teeth and kind of walk away. That's part of it [caregiving]. Like I said, I hope I don't do that when I get old, but I'm sure I will, unless I drop over with my boots on."

Burden was mentioned by a working couple early in the interview.

I later asked them if they could tell me about any burdensome experience they had. The wife replied, "I guess when my father-in-law was extremely sick . . . everyone was leaning on me because I was the main caretaker. Then one day when I got up in the morning, I could not stop crying. I suppose it was because my nerves were shattered. I was losing my father-in-law, and my husband's sister was home at the time, so I was trying to teach her to help me because father needed to be lifted. My husband's mother was not well at the time. She was having seizures and was on medication and that was an added burden. Those were really tough days; it was so difficult."

One couple thought I was asking about financial help when I asked, "Was there any **extra burden** placed on you as a couple because of the caregiving?"

Wife: "Well, a little bit, but not much. They've [elders] been pretty much on their own. We didn't have to do a lot. We did some buying, probably because it was more convenient, rather than take their checkbooks, I'd use mine. It was more of a convenience than it was a necessity." Then, she turned to her husband, "What do you think?"

Husband: "They were pretty much self-sufficient."

Wife: "You'd have to help them once in a while."

Husband: "You'd have to do some financial stuff for them."

Wife: "Like go pay their taxes with their own money; that kind of thing. You paid bills with their money. The small things we paid were a matter of convenience rather than financial obligation. We were fortunate that way. For some people it's a whole other thing when they have to take on the financial burden of caregiving."

Husband: "Well, I think in time your parents could become a financial burden because they are living to an older age and at a point they could outlive their money. So far they are taking good care of themselves."

Wife: "In the nursing home, they have nursing home insurance. . . . They take care of themselves as well as can be expected."

None of the couples I interviewed mentioned having to support their parents with financial help. When extra financial help was need for caregiving, it was covered by the elders, insurance, or government programs.

Summation

Common sense is needed to establish good family relationships for successful caregiving. Couples that had conflict, stress, or burden worked it out with good communication skills, patience, sensitivity, tact, cooperation, emotional awareness, networking, or just "letting it be." These positive attitudes, established before and during the caregiving experience, were key ingredients for successful caregiving.

Chapter Chuckle:

You know you are getting older when . . .

- You walk with your head held high, trying to get used to your bifocals.
- You turn out the lights for economic reasons instead of romantic ones.
- You remember today that yesterday was your wedding anniversary.

"No, no major things have changed. It just seems like it's [caregiving] part of everyday life. You just take it as it comes and deal with it when it comes."

Chapter 6

Personality Changes and Growth

Chapter Goal: To help caregivers understand the personality characteristics that are needed and the attitudes that will develop these characteristics so the caregiving experience can be successful.

What do you mean, changes?
    This question was sometimes asked when I confronted the couples with the question on personality changes and growth. Most of the people interviewed were very humble and had a difficult time talking about their own personalities. One wife remarked, "Probably an outsider could see it better than we can." She was right; outsiders may have noticed personality changes more than the spouses had. Some areas concerning personality changes and growth that emerged during the interviews included
- Changes in attitudes, interests, and knowledge
- Changes in personality due to aging
- Changes in personality due to caregiving
- Growth in psychological well-being
- Growth in personality due to achievement
- Growth in life-satisfaction

    A large majority of those interviewed did not feel their personalities had changed since the caregiving began; however, all of them gave examples of how their **attitudes, interests, and knowledge** had changed because of the caregiving experience. This contradiction may be due to the lack of understanding about what makes up the personality. One person thought the question was asking her if she became a different person. She replied, "It didn't change the way I am, it just changed our lifestyle at times." I tried to clarify the question by explaining that attitudes, interests, and knowledge are personality characteristics that can grow and change. This explanation brought forth many examples of changes experienced by those interviewed. **The most often cited changes were more patience, added sensitivity toward others and toward elders' needs, continued growth in knowledge and experiences, and reinforcement of moral reasoning and spirituality.** Other more precise changes that were cited were developing more tolerance, becoming a better person, slowing down, developing different priorities, being more compassionate, having more appreciation of life, being less selfish, becoming a stronger person, learning to accept one's own mortality, being more fulfilled, having a different outlook on life, changing some interests, growing up, appreciating a valuable opportunity, learning more about what older people think and need, getting along with elders, and growing in family togetherness.

The **attitudes** of these couples toward caregiving were generally good before, during, and after the caregiving. All attitudes that changed because of the caregiving experience were positive and showed growth in the individuals and the caregiving they did. One attitude that permeated most of the interviews was, "There's a time and a season for all things." I believe that these couples accepted their destinies and served with grace and honor.

Personal interests did not change much during the caregiving. Several couples expressed the opinion that they may have done a few other activities ~ like travel more ~ if they had not been caregiving, but felt that caregiving was more important. They had no regrets about that decision. One couple stated that now that the caregiving was over, they didn't know what to do in their spare time because caregiving took up all their spare time.

Almost half of those interviewed reported growth in their personalities due to **knowledge** obtained during the caregiving experience. Many felt this was a learning experience and expressed pride in their achievements. A wife commented, "It gives you insight because you know everything there is out there [about caregiving]." The couples that had completed the experience ~ some were still doing the caregiving ~ were very happy they had accepted the challenge and remained steadfast until the end. No one that had completed the experience expressed regret in what they had done or stated they would never do it again. One husband made a very profound statement about the **learning experiences** in caregiving: "One thing we've learned about all this is what it's like to get old. You not only learn what it's like, but you can *see* what it's like." Hands-on experience was very valuable for many caregivers in learning about their own aging and mortality, which will help define their own personalities when they became the care recipients.

Some individuals felt their **personalities had changed because of the aging process** ~ not the caregiving. One wife stated, "We all change, we're not in as big a hurry as we once were. Your priorities change." A husband stated, "It [caregiving] may have had some effect, but I think it's just more or less the process of aging that has changed us."

A few individuals believed that their **personalities had changed because of the caregiving.** A working husband replied, "I'm sure I'm a different person than if I'd not have had parents to take care of. It's a great experience. I might even wish for it; I know that." Another wife answered, "Yes, it did. It opened my eyes to realize that it's hard to live in a body that doesn't work, and I thank God every day, when I get up, that I can move around and take care of myself."

All of the individuals interviewed seemed to have excellent **psychological well-being.** Only one wife mentioned that a health care provider had advised her to take a break from the caregiving at one point in the process because it was affecting her health. Others mentioned that they took breaks from the caregiving occasionally because they realized they needed to get away from the caregiving for a while to renew their commitment and strength. Since all the caregivers had access to extended networks of caregivers, these networks were used when respite care was needed.

Growth in their personalities and **improved self-esteem** came through loud and clear in most of their statements. Many showed a great sense of pride when they talked about keeping their parents out of the nursing homes as long as possible.

Life-satisfaction was satisfactory for all the couples when they started the caregiving and remained good throughout the caregiving. No one expressed regret or wished their lives had been different. Some expressed sadness because the elder(s) they took care of had been very ill and needed intensive care. Several felt that caregiving was an opportunity to become a better person and promote life-satisfaction. An outspoken wife explained, "I think anyone that doesn't have that opportunity [caregiving] really misses out on something."

The personalities of these caregivers were kind, gentle, patient, respectful, humble, thoughtful, loving, and caring ~ ideally suited for caregiving.

Going to the source

All of the couples discussed some factors that showed how they had changed some of their attitudes about caregiving and life in general during their years of caregiving. The following vignettes will give you some insight into these changes.

Changes in **attitude, interests, and knowledge** were often discussed. Many caregivers said they had gained more **patience** and **sensitivity.**

Wife: "I think the thing I had to learn is patience. I used to be a very impatient person. I also had to learn not to be offended by what someone [elder] said because in two minutes that person, my mother, wouldn't remember what she'd said. She could say something hurtful ~ not meaning it ~ and then forget what she'd said. Just the way she phrased something came out wrong. You had to tell yourself, *'Well now, that wasn't what she meant, so I'm not going to take that personally.'*"

Question: "Are you saying that you learned not to be as sensitive?"

Wife: "Right. You're more sensitive to others, but not as personally sensitive. You start to read them like a child and that's what they need, even if they aren't saying it."

Question: "Am I hearing that you kind of got out of yourself and your own needs and got more into the elder's needs?"

Wife: "Yes ~ trying to stay one step ahead. You can't be a step behind in that situation. You have to be a step ahead to keep your own life in some sort of structure. It wasn't always easy."

Question: [to the husband] "What about you?"

Husband: "At times you get a little frustrated. I don't think I was ever offended with what anybody said or did to me. I just kind of took it as it came."

Wife: "His mother never would offend. She never got to that stage. She always said, *'Oh I hate to keep bothering you.'* That was her attitude so she never was that type."

Husband: "She felt as bad about her getting old as I felt." (This couple obviously had different experiences with their mothers.)

Opportunity, religion, mortality, and moral reasoning were mentioned by different couples as factors that caused positive changes.

A farm couple felt that caregiving was an **opportunity** to do something positive with their lives and understand their own **mortality**. I asked if the experiences they went through while caregiving helped them to understand elderly people better. The husband quickly answered, "Yes."

Question: "Can you elaborate on that?"

Husband: "Oh, I don't know. It's just something that we were thankful we could do. There are lots of children ~ they are away and have their jobs ~ that don't have the opportunity or chance to take care of their family. Then, I suppose there are some that wouldn't want to; I'm sure of that."

Question: "That's interesting that you consider this to be an opportunity."

Husband: "Well, like the bible says, you are supposed to respect your elders, so we grew up with that idea."

Question: "Interests in family caregiving were there before this elder care started, and these interests are still present?"

Husband: "Yes."

Question: "Those interests have been reinforced; they haven't changed?"

Husband: "Yes."

Question: [to his wife] "How about you?"

Wife: "Yes. We were basically real close to our parents anyway. We did a lot of things together. Like I said, everything else got left out and we just took care of parents instead of going and doing things for ourselves. It probably made us better people for ourselves as well as those being cared for."

Question: "Would you say this was a growth experience?"

Husband: "Yeah. We appreciated the opportunity to deal with caregiving."

Another wife's reply to changes in **attitudes or interests** was, "The thing is, when you take care of someone like that, you start to think that you are probably next in line. I think you probably appreciate things more. As much as we missed him [father] when he passed away, it was a relief, and then you feel a little guilty about thinking that way. But you know that you might be next ~ I'm sure glad that we did it."

I asked a very sincere couple, "Do you think there were any changes in your personalities in the last 20 years since your mother moved here, and you went through the process of caregiving?"

Husband: "I can't notice anything. I can't think of anything specific. I think the word patience is probably a word you could think about. It [caregiving] helped me to be more patient and have more patience with others."

Question: "All others not only elders?"

Husband: "Yes."

Question: "How about your interests? Have they changed any because of this experience?"

Wife: "I feel sorry for anybody that goes through this Alzheimer's thing. Caring for a person that has lost their mental ability ~ well, even lost the fact that you're their kid ~ they don't realize you are there. Right now, Mom never looks at us. When we go up and hug her and tell her we love her, then every once in a while a light goes on and she'll say, *'I love you, too, honey.'* This is really rare. It just lifts your spirits so much when it happens." (Both spouses were showing a lot of sad emotion at this point of the interview.)

Question: "Did your **moral reasoning** change any because of the caregiving?"

Husband: "Someone once said that it's hard to grow old. People fight it. They like to retain their youth. I guess it's [caregiving] helped me personally, when I see Mom and the process she's going through ~ to grow old more gracefully ~ in a sense."

Question: "As we grow older, caregiving helps us realize our own mortality?"

Husband: "Yes."

Some of the individuals felt that their **personalities had changed more because of aging** than because of the caregiving experience. Here are a few of their comments:

Question: "Looking at yourself now and twenty years ago, do you think you've changed?"

Husband: "From this experience or in general?"

Question: "Through this experience, we probably all change normally as we age."

Wife: "We all change. Like now ~ we have a new granddaughter ~ I could be home cleaning, but if my daughter wants me to come to her place and see a new tooth, I go and see a new tooth. Your priorities change."

Question: "So you think you've changed but it probably would of happened anyway?"

Wife: "Oh, yes. It's part of getting older. I'm a grandparent!" (This was said with pride.)

A similar answer for the question about caregiving as a factor that changed their personalities came from a couple who told many stories about how caregiving had been a **natural process** for them since they were first married.

Question: "Caregiving is like a continuous part of your life cycle ~ something done in your family generation after generation?"

Husband: "Yes, it's just become part of our life. We're in our sixties, and there are lots of our neighbors and friends going to Arizona during the winter. Well, we are in the same yard with our grandchildren. Right now, they [grandchildren] will sit on Grandpa's lap, when they get older they won't do that. If I'm not here to enjoy it right now, I'll miss that."

Wife: "Yes, it's the natural thing to do."

A good comment on change as a **natural life process** came from a farmer's wife who worked off the farm. "We've lived here for 30 years and we've grown old along with Grandma and Grandpa. To accept the fact that they are in their twilight years now, this is meant to be, this is life, old age, to just accept it, this is the way it is. We are thankful that they moved ~ this fall ~ into the home and that they could move together. They didn't have to split up ~ that was a big thing. Emotionally, that helped us all out because when they did have to move they could move together. As far as my own outlook on life, there have been no changes; it just reinforced my feelings that there is a time and season and there are chapters in our lives. . . . . We're in our fifties now so we look at things differently than when we were younger. It's [caregiving] part of life. It really has not changed my outlook on life. It's just reinforced my resolve. It's part of the process. We [spouses] are going through this together. It isn't abnormal. It's just the process."

A few couples mentioned that **caregiving experiences had changed** some of their **personality characteristics**. A small town couple was asked, "Did this experience give you more insight, change your personalities in any way?"

Wife: "Well, I'm more concerned and sensitive toward elderly people, specially those in nursing homes."

Question: "Has it changed you personally in any way? Made you different?"

Wife: "Probably more compassionate."

Question: [to her husband] "How about you?"

Husband: "I think I'm more thankful for nursing homes." [an attitude change]

A younger couple was asked, "Did this experience have some affect on you personally?"

Wife: "Yes, it did. It's awful, people don't know, you don't realize how hard it is for a person [elder] that can't do anything. It made me be more thankful for what I can do."

Question: "So it made you more sensitive toward the elderly and what they go through and also appreciate your own life and what you can do?"

Wife: "Definitely."

Husband: "Well, it's easy to sit here and say that I wouldn't want to put that responsibility on my kids, but I don't know if I'd want my kids to really look after me as much as we did them [elderly parents]. You can say it's pretty easy to have them [elders] go to a nursing home, but I still think we went beyond our means quite a bit."

Wife; "I do, too. Too much maybe, but I'm glad we did it."

Husband: "I'm glad we did it too. I guess some people expect their kids to take care of them. At this point I don't expect our kids to take care of me."

This couple got off the subject of personality change but revealed some personality characteristics as they answered the question. They were both committed to the caregiving of their parents but didn't want to put their own kids through that experience. They didn't realize that their kids needed that experience to become the kind, caring, nurturing, content people that they were.

Although one wife felt she hadn't changed because of the caregiving, her husband felt he had.

Husband: "I think you want to put these experiences back here [points to his brain] because someday we will be like my dad and mom. Let's hope we can understand when our children say, *'I don't know if you two should be driving anymore.'* By the same token, make sure that we don't rely on them for a lot of things that aren't necessary when we get older."

Question: "So I'm hearing you say it helped you realize your own aging and mortality?"

Husband: "Yes, some days you thought about that. We certainly can't be critical because it's just a matter of years before we're all going to be old."

Wife: "Walk in someone else's moccasins."

Husband: "Soon, we'll need our children to help us do some things, and they are going to ask us to do some things, too."

Question: "It probably made you a more sensitive person toward aging elders?"

Husband: "Yes, I think so."

All of the couples seemed to have excellent **psychological well-being;** however, few understood that I was asking about their feeling concerning their own inner psychological well-being. When asked, "Would you say your psychological well-being, the way you feel about yourself and your emotions, got better or worse during the caregiving," one wife's lengthy answer explains this confusion: "I think I understand and tolerated older people better now. When I'm around them, I think I should be helping them. In fact, if we move to town, I'd like to help take care of other older people and drive them to the doctor because some of these people don't have families around anymore. Having been there, I can see that there is a need for that. We have a guy in town that must be about 95, and he has no family here, so people have to get off work to help him. I would like to do something where I could take people to the doctor and check on them. I can see how, if you live a distance away, you can't do these things for your parents ~ to see when Dad gets up or take him a bowl of soup when he gets sick."

This wife had obviously come through the caregiving experience with wonderful inner psychological well-being but didn't know how to explain that feeling except by stating how she wanted to continue doing caregiving with others. Maybe her explanation showed me exactly how someone with positive psychological well-being would emerge from the caregiving experience.

Another wife thought her **psychological well-being** was better because of the caregiving she had done.

Wife: "Yes, you appreciate more of what you got. Last winter, we went away for the first time. We really enjoyed it. Makes you **appreciate things** more because you know you are heading in that direction [old age]."

Question: "You both seem to have gotten through this experience very well?"

Wife: "Oh, yes."

Question: "You don't seem to express any bitterness?"

Wife: "Oh, no."

Question: "You have a good sense of humor?"

Wife: "We laugh a lot."

Another wife had mentioned becoming more patient earlier in our interview. I then asked her if she could think of any other **psychological changes** that had happened to her.

Wife: "Well, I think psychologically you become more compassionate. Not only to your immediate family but to whoever is around."

Husband: "I guess when you see elderly people you used to think, *'They don't have to be doing this, or they could be doing something else.'* Now, you find out that they can't do things differently. They are probably doing the very best they can. When you see it happen, you say, *'That's just the way it is.'*"

Wife: "They [elders] just revert back to children in a lot of ways." (This couple had developed some pertinent insight into the aging process.)

Not all of the couples understood what **psychological well-being** meant; however, most tried to answer the question and some came up with some good answers.

Many couples had experienced **personality growth** because of their caregiving achievements and pride in a job well done. Not many individuals stated that they were proud of their accomplishments, but many showed pride through the stories they told or the body language they used when talking about their roles during the caregiving. One retired couple showed a lot of pride in their caregiving experiences because they had helped to take care of their father and mother in the elders' homes until the elders died. They didn't have to put their parents into nursing homes and this gave them a real sense of pride and increased their self-esteem.

Another husband **showed pride** in the caregiving he and his wife had done for both their mothers. He stated, "Just the idea that she wasn't going to the nursing home that quickly had a lot to do with it [feeling good about yourself and what had been done]."

Question: "Doing the best you could as long as you could made you feel good?"

Husband: "That's summing it up pretty good."

A son sounded **extremely proud** of the fact he was taking care of his parents.

Question: "It sounds to me like you felt you did your duty as a son and it turned out pretty good?"

Son: "Yes, I don't know if the word *duty* is right, it's just kind of that you're glad you can do it [caregiving]. I didn't feel obligated so much. I was proud I could do it."

The **life-satisfaction** for all these couples was very good. Here are some of their answers to the question, "Would you say your life-satisfaction is better or worse now because of this experience?"

Wife: "I think we're better people for it [caregiving]."

Husband: "You become more sensitive to elders' needs. You become more tolerant toward the elderly. At times elderly people can become rude, but you become more sensitive to what they are saying. If they say something that does offend you, you don't take it personally."

Question: "So, this sounds like it's really been a growth experience for you. It has enriched your lives?"

Wife: "It has for me." This wife went on to explain how she now enjoys going into nursing homes because her parents are there.

An older couple was asked, "Was your **life-satisfaction** good during the caregiving? Did you feel your life was fulfilled, and you had a lot of life-satisfaction?"

Wife: "I'm sure there were things we'd of liked to do that we didn't do."

Husband: "There are still a lot of things we'd like to do that we don't do." According to the husband's reply, even though the caregiving had ended, they still didn't do some of the things they talked about doing. The caregiving made no difference in their activity level.

I asked a working couple if this experience has given them more or less **life-satisfaction.**

Husband: "Oh, I think more because you see how you're vital to somebody; you're vital to your mother or parents. The satisfaction is that I'm here, and I can take care of her. Some young people nowadays virtually forsake their parents. They don't want anything to do with them. They don't want to see them grow old because that makes them feel like they are growing old. [Laughs] They don't want that responsibility. I've been blessed with the fact that I had that responsibility. I told Mom, *'You took care of me all your life; now I get to take care of you.'"*

Question: "Reciprocity?"

Husband: "Yes, I feel honestly that this isn't a very easy calling, but it's something I feel good about."

Question: [to his wife] "How about your life-satisfaction?"

Wife: "I know that there are a lot of jokes about mothers-in-law and everything, but I had a tremendous mother-in-law. Really, a tremendous mother-in-law. We did things together. We enjoyed the same things. We had prayer support between us. We could talk over things. I've really missed all that support. I'm here for her now. I just hope that she realizes that." What a wonderful statement about a mother-in-law who now has Alzheimer disease.

A farm couple was asked if they **were satisfied** with their lives during the caregiving, or if they would rather have been doing something different?

Wife: "I doubt we'd have done anything different."

Husband: "You always say you would have, but you never would. You kind of make up your mind pretty much as you go along in life, and you go ahead and do it. Something like caregiving doesn't change things."

A younger couple was asked if their **life-satisfaction** was good throughout the many years of caregiving. The husband very quickly and emphatically answered, "Absolutely!" His wife echoed these very same sentiments. This couple expressed in one word what the other couples seemed to feel. All of the couples thought their life-satisfaction was good throughout the caregiving because the caregiving was integrated into their everyday life.

Sufficient **life-satisfaction** will be the result for the caregivers, if there are **less family conflicts,** more **family adaptability** to roles and tasks, and **better decision making** processes that help **avoid stress** and **promote personal growth.** All of the factors discussed in this book are connected and **everything that goes around comes around.**

Summation

Personality change or growth is essential in promoting the integrity needed to accomplish successful caregiving. Attitudes of acceptance, openness, autonomy, and environmental mastery, along with a need for personal growth, a purpose in life, and self-acceptance were prominent in all of the couples interviewed. These essential ingredients helped promote successful caregiving.

Chapter Chuckle

You know you are getting old when . . .
- Your knees buckle, and your belt won't.
- You stop looking forward to your next birthday.
- Dialing long distance tires you out.

PART III

WHEN I'M AN OLD MAN
Author unknown

I'll ware mixed plaids.
I'll put my teeth in only when I need them.
I'll proudly and loudly produce massive amounts of phlegm at will.
I'll drive as slow as I want . . . I was here first, wasn't I?
I'll buy my grandchildren gifts my kids don't want them to have.
I'll let waiters and waitresses really know how "everything" is tonight.
I'll wear Vicks Vap-O-Rub, BenGay, and the Icy Blue stuff
instead of cologne.
I'll let my gut stick out. Way, way out . . . who gives a rip anymore?
I'll darn sure let people know what I think about
"the crap they're showing on TV these days."
I'll let my grandchildren get away with things I used to punish my
children for doing.
I'll blow my nose as hard and as loud as I want!
I'll make darn sure I get my "Senior" discount!

I'll refuse to stand in long grocery store lines to pay for a quart of milk and
a box of bran. If they catch me, I'll just act senile.
I'll darn sure let people know what I think about "the crap the government
makes us go through just to get what we have coming to us."
I'll keep my turn signal on as long as I want, dab nabit!
I'll pass gas whenever and wherever I dang well please.
I'll develop an addiction to Milk of Magnesia.
I'll write long letters to the editor about whatever I don't like.
I'll chug Metamucil like I used to chug beer.
I'll obsessively make elaborate contraptions to keep the
dang squirrels off my bird feeders.
I'll have more hair growing out of my nose and ears than
on the top of my skull.
I'll flirt with women who won't have gone out with me
even when I was their age.

I'll brush my eyebrow hair up over my bald spot.
I'll go to them all-you-can-eat buffet lunch places
and bring a doggy bag with me.
I'll wear my pants hiked up around my armpits,
or I'll let them ride comfortably down under my belly.
I'll blow my social security money by buyin' crap
from the back of books.
When I'm an Old Man.

"No, no major things [strategies] were used. It just seems like it's [caregiving] part of everyday life. You just take it as it comes and deal with it when it comes up."

Chapter 7

Strategies or Adaptations

Chapter Goal: To outline strategies or adaptations that promoted the attitudes needed to make the caregiving experience more tolerable while practicing successful caregiving.

What do you mean ~ coping strategies? Many individuals interviewed did not think they had used any strategies. They didn't understand the term "coping strategies." During the interviews many coping strategies came to light. These strategies or adaptations fell into the four broad categories discussed in Chapters 3, 4, 5, and 6.
- Strategies used to keep motivated
- Strategies used to help with roles and tasks
- Strategies used to promote better family relationships
- Strategies used to promote personal growth and change

Strategies for motivation
Coping strategies used to motivate couples included
- Using humor
- Networking
- Motivating spouses
- Keeping elders happy
- Setting a good example for children
- Showing equal affection to biological and in-law parents
- Taking things one day at a time

If you are starting to see a common thread running through all of these chapters, you are right. Every area of caregiving is related, and all areas focus on promoting good attitudes that help accomplish that area. Many of these attitudes overlap, as do strategies. For example: it is impossible to separate motivational strategies with strategies used to perform tasks more easily because you need to be motivated to perform most of the caregiving tasks. Also, if you are motivated, you will want better relationships with family members, which will in turn promote personal growth in all relationship areas. This whole book is a *which came first, the chicken or the egg?* conundrum. Everything relates to everything else, and the process goes around and around.

Having a good sense of humor was invaluable for all of the couples. They laughed a lot during the interviews. "These things [situations] would make my husband angry at first, but then we'd start talking about it and it was funny. You had to laugh at some of the things that happened. They were pretty cute."

Everyone made at least one funny statement during the interview ~ sometimes to cut the tension or sadness that was building as they told their stories. The husbands also liked to tease their wives. The wives would laugh at their statements.

- "I'd climb the walls at times." **(Laugh)**
- "Well, she gave me a black eye several times." **(Laugh)**
- "If I don't get along, she beats me." **(Laugh)**
- "When things would try your patience, you just had to **laugh** about them."
- "Some of the stuff that went on, you just had to **laugh** about it."

They told many humorous stories about themselves, their elders, and situations in general. These stories were told with respect, love, and emotion. Some laughed with tears in their eyes. Most spouses worked together when telling their funny stories. After telling about some of the sad things that they had been through, a husband summed up the aging process with a humorous statement: "The person that dreamed up *Golden Years* must have been nuts. I don't know where he got that from!"

Let me share some of these stories with you. A son told a story about his dad that showed a strategy [to keep his father healthy and happy] he used along with humor. "At this particular time, when we are here in North Dakota, I have a little strategy going with him [elderly father]. I tell him to come over from my sister's house to watch baseball at my house so he gets out and walks a little."

I repeated his statement and elaborated on it. "So to get him to exercise more you get him to watch baseball at your house so he walks back and forth between houses?" He agreed and laughed; then he added,

"I tell him if he'd run, it wouldn't take him so long!" (Humor was used by the son to promote a more healthy life style for the father.)

Another son told about his elderly father who loved to farm and always wanted to help. "We would worry about him when he was out there on the tractor. We had to give him a field to work in where he couldn't get into too much trouble!" (This strategy used humor to keep the elder motivated.)

When discussing sensitivity toward elders, a wife told a story about not being offended by older people. "Yes, you don't take it [what elders say] personally. There is an old guy in town that is borderline rude. He thinks he can say what he wants to, and now I've learned to humor him. Before I might have said, *'I don't need this! I'll just leave,'* now I kind of roll it off." Her husband quickly added. "I occasionally leave!" (A strategy to prevent stress.)

Driving by elders was a topic of many humorous stories. We were discussing an elderly father's driving when the wife said, "He drove very slowly, never stopping at stop signs." The husband continued, "One day I followed him when he went through a stop sign. I told him about it when we got home, and he said, *'Well, the guy behind me did, too.'*" (A strategy to help accept role reversal.)

Another funny driving story was told by a retired son. "He [father] had a little trouble with his car. It wouldn't steer right, according to him, so I asked him, *'What's the matter?'* He said, *'Well, I'm driving down the road, and when I look out there [at the scenery] the car comes across the yellow line.'*" (Elders need to continue driving to be independent and motivated. To put up with some elders' driving habits took a lot of humor.)

Another couple told several stories about their mother when she was in the nursing home. It seems that the staff had asked if there was anything they could do to make the elderly mother happy. The son replied, "She likes to help ~ like wash dishes." So when the staff baked, they would let the mother help do dishes. This made the mother very happy. Later the staff told the son that there was only one problem with this arrangement. Whenever they put the mixing spoon down, the mother grabbed it and washed it, so they had to keep getting new spoons to complete the baking project. (A strategy to keep the elder happy.)

There were humorous stories told with love and tears about elders who had lost some of their mental ability. When I asked one son if his father was more difficult to take care of when he became senile, the son answered, "He wasn't more difficult; it was easier. I didn't even realize that he didn't know who I was. When my sister came and stayed with him [to replace the son for a few days] he [father] said, *'Who's that guy staying with me? I think he's going to kick me out of this house.'* My sister said, *'That's your son!'* He just looked surprised." (Humor was needed here to motivate the caregivers to continue their work.)

Stories were told about in-laws as well as parents. One wife told a funny story about her mother-in-law. "Our church starts at 9:30 Sunday morning, so she always says *'You come and get me.'* She lives thirteen miles away, so I told her driving all those miles that early in the morning was hard. She said, *'Go to bed earlier.'*" (A strategy to help accept the demands of elders.)

A wife told about her elderly father-in-law who liked his food very hot. "He loved the microwave. He kept warming things up until the food got tough. I told him, *'Grandpa, you can't warm food up so much because the microwave will make it tough.'* He kept right on warming the food up and complaining it was tough." (The strategy here was to treat in-laws, with the same affection and humor that you treated your biological parents.)

Stories were told about cute things the elders would say and do. A daughter told a story about how her mother only allowed her to buy a few pills each week. The mother watched her medication very closely. She [elder] said, *"I might not live long enough to use it up."* (Understanding the elder was the strategy used here.)

Another elderly mother had broken her hearing aid. The children wanted to get her a new one. "*'Oh, no,'* mother said, *'I hear plenty good.'* A friend stopped in to visit mother one day and heard her TV blasting away down the hall before she got to mother's apartment. After we heard about this incident, we bought her a new hearing aid. The next time we visited mother, she said, *'I hear things I've never heard before. I can hear the furnace kick in at night!'* We turned on her TV and she said, *'Turn it down, it's so loud it's going to take the top of my head off!'*" (Networking was a strategy that helped this family solve a problem for their mother.)

When asked if they would expect their children to help them someday, a husband replied, "I think so, yeah. Our children know about the care we are giving Mom and Dad. I told them, *'Pay attention! You're going to have to take care of us someday!'*" (Setting examples for children was a strategy that motivated caregivers.)

While talking about lessons learned, a son commented, "When I was talking about the things Dad would do that would make me want to pull my hair out, I had to stop and think, *'Well, I have done just as many things when I was young where he sat there and said, 'What the &%$#* are you doing?'"* (Understanding the elder's frustration was a strategy used by this son.)

One son spoke with love and pride [showing affection] as he told stories about his dad. This son said his elderly dad wouldn't go to the Senior Citizen's Center because, according to the elder, *'There's nothing there but old people.'"* This same son told how his dad died shortly after he was put into a nursing home. "He was having little strokes, I think. He got up one morning and went on the exercise bike. He went to lie down for a nap afterwards and never got up. How lucky can you be? He died with his boots on!" (I think this son would like to die with his boots on someday. Thinking about his own mortality with humor was a strategy used by this son.)

A husband was relating all the things he'd learned by watching his mother go through Alzheimer's disease. He summed up his statement by saying, "I hope all I've learned [by watching his mother age] will help me in my own aging experience." His wife looked at him with a sweet smile and said, "I hope it does, too." (Motivating her spouse with humor was the strategy used by this wife.)

All of the couples used humor as a strategy to help them get through their many years of caregiving. They could see the humor in almost any situation and also knew how to laugh at themselves.

Networking with others was an important strategy used by a large majority of the couples. "It was a united front . . . a caring, united front," was a statement made by a wife that expressed the need for good networking to keep motivated. I noted that the larger the network of caregivers, the more motivated the couples were. Networks included children, siblings, relatives, neighbors, church members, and community organizations.

The following dialogue depicts the use of networking by a younger couple, who felt that networking was necessary to continue caregiving.

Husband: "Well, I don't think it's [caregiving] for anybody to tackle unless they have extra help. One person couldn't do it alone. If one person is going to take care of another person, they would have to live with them. If you have several to help out, it's not such a burden."

Wife: "We had lots of help."

Husband: "It wasn't that any individual got too bogged down with it [caregiving]."

Question: "So you would advise others to definitely have a network of helpers to keep you motivated?"

Wife: "Uh-huh."

Husband: "Some people can't do that [have an extended network of caregivers]. I tell you if they can't, they are taking on a lot if they want to take care of somebody [elder]."

Using nursing homes was a networking strategy used by many couples when the caregiving became too intense to continue in the home. "It wasn't easy toward the end. We got pretty upset ~ not because she had to have all this care ~ I think it bothered us because we knew she had to go into a nursing home. We didn't want to put her there. We did not! But as the tasks got harder to do, it made it easier for us to do that [use a nursing home]."

Keeping your spouse motivated was another part of the strategy equation mentioned by a majority of the couples. Suggestions for keeping spouses motivated [mostly by women] were

- Talking calmly
- Supporting
- Reasoning
- Consoling
- Reassuring
- Listening
- Showing appreciation
- Counseling
- Taking turns

Women appreciated the support of their husbands and in many cases had to keep the husbands motivated to get the support they needed. All of the husbands supported the caregiving, but they were not as verbal about their feelings as the wives were.

The following dialogue shows how religion and teamwork went hand in hand for one couple.

Wife: "The thing I guess is ~ we know that our Lord is always with us. He gives us the strength that we need and that is the most important thing. Sometimes when you were very, very stressed, when you were caring for older people, and sometimes when you felt they're not happy with what you are doing ~ it's a tough situation. We [husband and wife] stuck together."

Question: "Worked as a team?"

Wife: [laughs] "Consoled each other if there were any problems."

All types of strategies were used to **keep elders happy.** Most of the couples felt that keeping their care recipient happy was a major key to successful caregiving. Some of the strategies used to keep elders happy, besides teamwork and cooperation by the caregivers, were

- Work out a daily schedule that included fun activities for the elder.
- Enjoy your parents before they need intensive caregiving, and you'll enjoy them more when they become very frail.
- Motivate the elders to do chores and social activities.
- Try seeing things from the elder's point of view.
- Think of elders as people who took care of you and have always been there for you.
- Show affection to the elders, and they will return that affection.
- Keep the elders at home as long as possible, so they know you did everything you could do before you put them into a home.

About half way through one interview, I summed up what a working couple had been saying. "Some of the strategies I'm hearing are that you cooperated as a team, and you tried to see situations from the elders point of view. Are there any other strategies that you'd like to mention?"

Husband: "I'd like to say that you try to remember what she'd [elder] like to do. She liked to see things. She liked to shop and go for rides out in the country. She liked birds and wildlife. We'd go to farms and watch them work. We arranged times when we'd take off a week and go to her home state and visit all the places where she used to live. She really enjoyed that."

Question: "It sounds like something that really motivated you folks was seeing her happy?"

Husband: "Yes. It pleasured her [elder] to go out and go for a ride. When we were kids, and Dad was in the service, Mom used to take us kids in the car, and we'd go down town and watch the people go by. She liked to do that, so that's what we do now."

This couple suggested that the elderly enjoy the simple things in life. A good strategy is to find out what the elder likes to do. Most of the time it is something simple ~ just spend time with them and let them relive old memories.

Setting an example for their children was a goal for many couples as well as a strategy. A farm wife said it best: "In about ten years we'll be there, too, so I hope our kids do for us what we're doing for our parents. You can see traits that you are getting that your parents had, so you know it's part of the cycle of life." That same sentiment was echoed by many of the couples. To keep the caregiving ethic going from generation to generation was a very important motivational strategy for many couples. Strategies used to involve children in the caregiving of elderly grandparents were

- Ask them to do little things like take the elders shopping.
- Make them feel that they are an important part of the caregiving equation.
- Let them do tasks that they are trained to do. Example: a grandson who was an electrician helped his grandparents with problems in that area.
- Praise them for the work they do to help with the caregiving.

Affection shown to spouses, children, elders, or anyone involved with the caregiving was an excellent strategy used by everyone to help improve and maintain good conditions during caregiving. The word "love" was used many times to express feelings about different individuals involved in the caregiving. Affection was used in humor to motivate spouses, to keep elders happy, to set a good example for children, and even to network with friends and relatives. Affection, kindness, and thoughtfulness went a long way to promote strategies of all kinds.

An attitude of taking things **one day at a time** was an important strategy for many couples. One couple combined resolve and priority when discussing their caregiving philosophy. The husband started the conversation: "Put it in the back of your mind that you have to do this [caregiving], and if there is something you don't like, you just do it and don't say anything." His wife agreed with him. He continued, "You bit your lips or tongue, whatever you call it. Whether you're working at another job or anything else, you know what has to be done, and you do it; whether you like it or not . . . you take things one day at a time."

Section Summation

Humor was used throughout all the interviews to answer questions. Humor was a big strategy used by all of the couples. To keep motivated to continue caregiving year after year, it was necessary to have good motivational strategies that promoted networking, kept elders happy, set good examples for future caregivers, showed affection, and kept spouses motivated. Taking the caregiving one day at a time helped prevent stress and worry over situations that the caregivers had no control over.

Strategies for roles and tasks

The adaptations needed to perform tasks and roles that were mentioned most often were in conjunction with

- Doing traditional tasks
- Clarifying roles and tasks
- Using help from extended networks
- Promoting flexibility at work
- Accepting co-residency

Strategies suggested to make caregiving roles and tasks easier were

- Keeping the elders in their own homes and letting them do their own work as long as possible so they feel independent
- Doing the tasks you do best and are most comfortable doing
- Putting each spouse in charge of final decisions for their own parents
- Setting boundaries for roles and tasks that are understood by both spouses
- Working together as a team
- Setting priorities as a family
- Making schedules the whole family could live with
- Letting elders help with chores whenever possible
- Working caregiving tasks into regular visits with elders so they don't feel that they are an extra burden on the caregiver
- Networking with all types of extended family, church, and community help
- Moving in with parents [co-residence] if long distances made it difficult to do caregiving
- Seeking outside services (nursing homes, home health aid, etc.) when intensive care or respite care was needed

Some adaptations made by wives to make their tasks easier were
- Preparing food ahead of time and freezing it for future use
- Being well-organized and planning ahead
- Sorting medicines used by elders a week ahead of time so the elders can help themselves
- Using convenience foods and restaurants

All of the wives did **traditional tasks,** and the majority of the husbands did traditional work. This arrangement worked best for the couples because they were better at doing traditional tasks, and they felt more comfortable doing traditional jobs. Some of the husbands would do non-traditional tasks for their parents or when their wives were gone. Some wives did non-traditional tasks when necessary to keep the caregiving running smoothly. Being able to do tasks they were good at gave the caregivers a sense of pride and self-esteem, which in turn kept them motivated to do the caregiving.

A husband told about a task he did because he was stronger than his wife: "The last time he stayed with us, he didn't have a car, so we had to take him around when he wanted to go someplace. At different times he had a hard time getting up a couple stairs, so we had to help him up and down the stairs. He took care of himself otherwise." I then asked him if he helped the father get up and down the stairs because he was physically stronger than his wife. He answered, "Yes, Dad was getting so that he'd come off those steps like he was running, so I'd make sure I was there to catch him if he fell."

Clarification of roles and tasks was a prominent theme in all the interviews. Everyone knew what they needed to do, performed what they did best, took turns, and helped with non-traditional jobs when their spouses were busy. All caregivers were in charge of final decision making for their own parents, even if some wives were the primary caregivers for their in-laws. This worked out best because no one wanted the final word on what to do about elderly in-laws.

Setting boundaries worked for one couple. This couple had mentioned throughout the interview that they each took care of their own parents, since both sets of parents needed caregiving at the same time. I asked them, "Did either of you help the other when there was an emergency?"

Husband: "Yes."

Wife: "Not very much though. I took care of my folks, and he took care of his."

Husband: "I only helped her once in a while, when there was something she couldn't do alone, like the time I sawed down a tree branch at her folk's house after a storm."

Question: "So each spouse took care of their own parents?" (They both nodded *yes* in agreement to my question.) "Can you think of anything else you did?"

Wife: "We didn't have any planned strategy, it [caregiving] just flowed naturally. He did what he did best, and we pretty much were independent of each other." (Setting boundaries and keeping their own independence was an understood strategy.)

Extended networks helped all of the couples with caregiving. These networks were flexible and provided care services when the couples could not be present. A vast majority of couples cited cooperation from caregiver networks ~ extended family, church members, and community people ~ as primary strategies for performing roles and tasks effectively over long periods of time.

One story about networking was told by a mother of three daughters. This mother had to be gone for long periods of time: "I taught our girls how to cook. They each had to pick out one night a week, whichever one they wanted, and do the cooking. They also had to take turns packing their father's lunch for work each day."

I asked a working couple if they used an extended network to help. The husband answered first, "Well, people from the church have been very helpful. When we're gone on a vacation or go to see our kids, they help. There have been times when they have gone over to her apartment and checked in on her." His wife added, "Before she was in the nursing home." He continued, "Before she was in the home . . . payed a call on her just to see how she was and if there was anything she needed. A couple of ladies took her shopping ~ took her for a ride ~ people from the church. She lived in a place where there were many older ladies, and they all kind of took care of each other, too."

Almost half of the caregivers had **flexibility in their jobs** because they were self-employed, worked part-time, didn't work outside their homes, or were retired. Flexibility helped them adapt their work schedules to the caregiving. Having the time to do the caregiving motivated the caregivers to do the tasks necessary to be successful caregivers. The people interviewed also reported flexibility in schedules and lifestyles as positive factors that promoted easier role adaptations and task completions. Those that worked full-time also made adaptations in their work, such as letting fellow employees help when they had to leave and having good substitutes when they had to be gone from work.

The following dialogue sums up the strategies in this section very well. Both spouses were working at the time the caregiving began, but things changed as time went on.

Wife: "I worked when we first moved to town to help Dad out. I worked nights, so it didn't interfere with anything."

Question: "So, there was a time when you were working and caregiving at the same time, but then you eventually gave that up?"

Wife: "Yes, I gave that up and became a full-time homemaker."

Husband: "She volunteers work at the nursing home, too."

Wife: "Oh, yes. For one thing this was a time of our life when we would have been gone a lot more, but now we couldn't. We went to see our daughter once, and we wanted to extend our trip, but we felt we just couldn't stay any longer. We had to get home because Dad was waiting patiently for us to come home. We never went anyplace for more than two weeks. My brother-in-law would look after Dad when we did go away. . . . I think I also cooked differently. I cooked larger meals, and then I would portion the food up and freeze it. Dad couldn't do much, especially the last two years. He could take food out of the freezer and reheat it. If I was going to be gone, I'd make sure things were done ahead of time."

Question: "It sounds like you were organized?"

Wife: "Yeah, things have to go pretty smooth or things get on my nerves if they don't go good."

Question: "Okay, you're very organized, very structured. Did you have a regular schedule that you would follow with your father?"

Wife: "The schedule was pretty much like any family, I think. We'd eat certain times, do laundry certain times, etc."

Question: [to her retired husband] "How about you? Did you make any adjustments?"

Husband: "Not too much. Not very much at all that I can think of. I was retired, so I had time to help. [To his wife] Can you think of anything?"

Wife: "No. Like we said, Father was a very social person at the beginning. When the town paper came out, all the social events for the coming week were written down, not only on his calendar but in his book. So we kind of scheduled things around that because I'd have to go with him. If we had something planned, we'd just change plans unless we couldn't. We went to our own functions, too, ~ weddings and such ~ we went to those, but I planned most of our schedules around the things Father wanted to do."

Co-residence was sometimes necessary. I mentioned to a couple that they had stated earlier in the interview that they sometimes lived with their mother. "How did that work?" I asked.

Husband: "Yes, in the winter time."

Wife: "Yes, there was co-residence at times."

Question: "Was that easier or harder?"

Husband: "Probably a lot easier."

Wife: "It was easier."

Husband: "Because we weren't going back and forth to our farm all the time. It's about 20 miles back and forth."

All of the couples were very resilient when adaptations were made to perform tasks and when their life's roles changed. Resilience was a key ingredient that helped them be successful caregivers.

Section Summation

Strategies for promoting traditional work were useful in preventing stress and promoting self-esteem. Strategies used to clarify roles and tasks helped prevent stress by setting boundaries that were realistic. Strategies for networking were necessary to prevent stress and assist in intensive care or respite care. Strategies used to produce flexibility in jobs and life style also prevented stress, gave caregivers time to do the caregiving, and made time to do things with elders. All of these strategies promoted harmony in the caregiving experience.

Strategies for better family relationships

Coping strategies used to avoid conflict and prevent stress during the caregiving experience that related to family relationships included

- Good communication skills
- Cooperation
- Emotional support
- Religious faith or spirituality and good moral reasoning
- Flexibility in thinking, lifestyle, and schedules

- Equal affection for biological and in-law parents

All of the couples felt that **good communication** among spouses, elders, and the extended network of caregivers was essential in preventing stress and conflict. A majority of couples mentioned communication as a strategy, and the rest implied that good communication was needed as they told their stories.

Strategies that were used to promote good communication were
- Learning to control anger ~ "Just don't get angry."
- Walking away ~ "Let it go."
- Compromise ~ "Give and take."
- Brainstorming ~ "I'd call my sister and we'd talk."
- Appreciation ~ "My brother would send me a little money, once in a while, to do something for myself."
- Sensitivity ~ "You had to watch what you'd say to them [elders]."

Being sensitive was a big factor for good communication. Trying to understand elders and learning about their needs helped promote sensitivity. Caregiving is a reminder that you are going to be there some day.

I noted that none of those interviewed mentioned a need to be sensitive to their spouse. They all seemed to be focused on their behavior toward the care recipient and didn't think of their partner when discussing this strategy. It was my opinion that all of those interviewed showed sensitivity toward their spouses during the interviews by taking turns, listening to each other, and respecting each other's opinions.

Promoting **cooperation** with all extended network members and especially siblings was an important strategy for a majority of the couple. When siblings helped with tasks or showed appreciation, couples expressed their gratitude in very emotional ways. "Our sisters and brothers, everybody, just got along so well. Everyone goes along with what the other suggests. You know, it works out really well."

Strategies used to promote cooperation included
- Using good communication skills ~ "We'd talk things out."
- Using tact ~ "Be careful how you said things. What you said and how you said it."
- Understanding ~ "We were the only two here capable of doing it. It's pretty hard to call a brother out of state and asked him to come home and do something."

- Being patient ~ "You need a lot of patience when working with the elderly. They don't move very fast."
- Being firm but fair ~ "Sometimes I just had to say, *'No, we're not going today.'*"

Patience was a very important strategy. Everyone talked about being patient to promote any aspect of caregiving. One husband defined patience: "Stay on a steady course ~ relax!" When all other attempts to be patient failed, "Sometimes you would have to kind of ignore them [elders], and they would go away" was a final solution for one husband. Two other statements that showed final attempts to be patient were "You just kind of fell in line," and "Grin and bear it."

One wife explained how she communicated with her husband when he would get angry with his father: "I'd just talk to my husband and say, *'Remember he's old,'* but I never talked to my father-in-law about it because I don't thing Dad would have known what I was talking about because he thought everything was just cool. He thought everything was just fine. I don't know if he recognized the stress that he caused between us once in a while. This wasn't constant ~ most of the time things were fine."

Emotional support from siblings, spouses, elders, and community members was an important strategy needed to prevent conflict and stress. Emotional support came in the form of
- Appreciation expressed to caregivers by others
- Compliments given to caregivers by others
- Reassurance given to caregivers by others

Those of you who support a primary caregiver need to continually show appreciation, give compliments and reassure the caregiver that you are thinking of them and are there to help. This will provide the emotional support they need to continue the caregiving.

The majority of couples appreciated any efforts made by anyone to show appreciation for what they were doing or had done. Having anyone tell them they were doing a good job was a boost to their morale. "He [elder] always bragged us up to other people" was said with pride by one caregiver. This same caregiver confessed, "It was a reward just having people compliment you on what you were doing." (Siblings of caregivers and care recipients take note.)

Compliments also helped relieve guilt, according to one wife. A friend had told her, "You're doing everything you can. It's just the way things are." This made her feel better about her situation. Church members were often cited as supporting couples and giving them many compliments. (Community members take note.)

For most couples where wives did more of the caregiving tasks than the husbands did, if the husbands gave their wives good emotional support, the wives always felt the couple shared equally in the caregiving. (Husbands take note.)

A strong **religious faith** produced good **moral reasoning,** which promoted good family relations. All of the couples indicated on a rating scale taken at the end of the interviews, that their religion or spirituality helped them cope with the caregiving experience; however, only half of the couples emphasized the importance of their religion or spirituality to overcome stress and conflict during the interview. I can only surmise that talking about religion or spirituality was a difficult thing for many, so they did not bring it up during the interview. One wife concluded, "I suppose in the long run it [religion/spirituality] played a part." When asked if his moral reasoning had changed because of the caregiving experience, one husband replied, "I don't think it changed. I think it was there before and is still there like it always was." (Chapter 8 discusses religion/spirituality in more detail.)

Flexibility in thinking, lifestyle, and schedules helped alleviate stress for many couples. Some strategies used to promote flexibility were

- Be open minded ~ "Try seeing things from their point of view."
- Take a break ~ "Sometimes we just had to get away for a while."
- Plan ahead ~ "I made a schedule each week, but sometimes it was broken. We did the caregiving first."

I asked a couple if they had any strategies for improving relationships, and they mentioned they had to **change their lifestyle and schedules.**

Wife: [laughing] "Oh, definitely. I mean there is no such thing as on Tuesday you get your hair done. You just do these things as you can. Especially with my parents. You never know what will happen next. If in the morning somebody has to go to the doctor ~ you go. I mean, this is getting pretty unpredictable. I mean, you needed a lot of flexibility with them [elders]."

Husband: "Things can change in a hurry."

Wife: "You can go to bed at night and by morning Mom is calling because Dad was sick all night. Sometimes, she didn't know how to use the phone [mother has Alzheimer's]. Dad would go to bed peacefully and wake up sick. It is so traumatic."

Question: "So flexibility is the key word in your situation?"

Wife: "Yes." [her husband nods, yes]

Another dialogue about **flexibility in thinking** was started when I asked a couple if they changed any of their ideas or thinking about relationships to help them deal with the caregiving? The wife quickly replied, "You always kind of change the way you think. You think that maybe if I suggest she [elder] do this or that differently things will change. You always do that. You always change your way of thinking."

Equal affection and care shown for all parents was a very important strategy used by these couples. None of the individuals interviewed said anything during the interviews that would indicate they loved their own parents more than the parents of their spouse. "I loved your folks," said by a daughter-in-law, and "We loved her," said by a daughter-in-law about her mother-in-law, were two of the many statements made by in-laws that showed affection. All of the spouses showed as much care and concern for their in-laws as they did their own parents by verbalizing their affection or showing this affection in their body language as they talked.

Section Summation

Good communication, sensitivity, patience, and emotional support lead to cooperation. Religion and spirituality promoted good moral reasoning, which was a result of putting more faith in their God, which promoted relaxation and contentment, which lead to more flexibility in thinking and lifestyle. As you can see, all of these strategies are related. You need to practice them all because one strategy will promote another strategy.

Strategies for personal growth and change

It was difficult for couples to think of any strategies they had used to promote positive personality changes and growth. It was obvious to me that all of the couples had grown in one or more areas of personality development during their caregiving experiences. It was easier for an outsider to evaluate areas of growth than it was for those that had been involved with the caregiving experience for a long period of time.

Strategies used by couples to **promote positive personality changes and growth** were compiled and outlined while reviewing the transcripts of the interviews and by direct observation. These strategies were clustered into four basic themes
- Strategies that promoted attitudinal changes
- Strategies that promoted psychological well-being
- Strategies that promoted life-satisfaction
- Strategies that reinforced and strengthened faith and religion

The majority of the couples mentioned strategies that brought about **attitudinal changes** that are now more positive because of the caregiving experience. These changes include
- A more positive view of elders ~ "We tried to look at it from her point of view."
- A more positive view of nursing homes ~ "I never used to like going to nursing homes, but now I don't mind it."
- A more positive view of the aging process ~ "You need to realize that you'll be there some day."
- A more positive view of co-residence with elders ~ "It was easier when we lived with her."
- A more positive view of caregiving in general ~ "It was hard, but I'm sure glad we did it."

All of these attitudinal changes brought about personality changes such as more patience, more tolerance, more sensitivity, and more knowledge, which in turn brought about growth in personality for many caregivers.

Strategies used by all of the couples to promote **psychological well-being** included
- Continuing all normal, everyday activities
- Being flexible
- Setting priorities
- Being tolerant
- Learning to be calm, cool, and content
- Showing compassion

Strategies that promoted **life-satisfaction** were obvious in all of the couples' lives because they all indicated their lifestyle was satisfactory during the caregiving experience. Strategies used by these couples to promote life-satisfaction included
- Reducing conflict

- Being adaptable
- Making good decisions
- Fostering autonomy or independence for elders
- Using family support systems
- Recruiting help from public service providers

I observed the pride felt by over half the caregivers when they spoke about accomplishing a variety of roles successfully. A majority of the couples suggested the need to learn and gain knowledge about caregiving had improved their life-satisfaction because they now were more knowledgeable and better prepared for their own aging.

A majority of couples admitted that their **religion/spirituality** had been strengthened or reinforced. One wife felt that her moral reasoning had been strengthened because caregiving was a learning process. The strengthening of their faith had promoted better **attitudes, quality of relationships, and morality.**

Section Summation

Attaining better attitudes, relationships, and morality promoted more psychological well-being and better life-satisfaction.

Here's the thing!

The biggest attitudinal change in most of these couples was their outlook concerning their own mortality. "The thing is, when you take care of someone like that [caregiving] you start thinking that you're probably next, and you appreciate everyday things more." Going through the caregiving helped them see what they would have to go through in the final stages of their life span. It made them more sensitive, patient, understanding, and accepting of their elders and the aging process. Caregiving showed them how to appreciate what they had in the present and to enjoy the time they had left in the future.

When looking at their own mortality, many of the caregivers started to appreciate nursing homes more. Many comments were made about going to nursing homes and visiting with all the old people in the homes. For example, one wife was asked, "Has your personality changed because of the caregiving?" She replied, "I think so. I mean, I've always taken it for granted that everybody gets another day older each day, but now I enjoy going to the nursing home and being around elderly people and doing for elderly people." Many of the people interviewed were probably thinking ahead to when they would be in nursing homes. They did not want to be put into homes and forgotten.

The most prominent personality characteristics I noticed in all these couples were how relaxed and calm they were. I commented to one couple, "You seem to be very relaxed and laid back people." They both laughed. Then I added, "This seems to be part of your personalities." The husband calmly responded, "We don't get excited about things." How right he was!

Chapter Summation

The four major areas of strategies that motivate, help with task completion, reduce stress and conflict, and promote personality growth or change are essential while maintaining good attitudes or establishing new attitudes that are needed for successful caregiving. Many of the individual strategies (patience, sensitivity, communication, cooperation, understanding, openness, flexibility, humor, affection, support, religion, etc.) overlap into all four of these major areas of successful caregiving. It is difficult to isolate one strategy into one area because each area affects all the other areas. The important thing to remember is that all of these strategies will promote better attitudes, which in turn will make caregiving more successful.

Chapter Chuckle

You know you are getting old when . . .
* Your back goes out more often than you do.
* "Happy Hour" is taking a nap.
* You burn the midnight oil until after 9:00 p.m.

PART IV

CRABBIT OLD WOMAN
By Phyllis McCormack
(An old woman in an English geriatric ward)

What do you see nurse, what do you see?
What are you thinking when you look at me?
A crabbit old woman, not very wise,
Uncertain of habit, with far away eyes.

Who dribbles her food and makes no reply;
Then you say in a loud voice, "I do wish you'd try."
Who seems not to notice the things that you do,
And forever is losing a stocking or shoe.

Unresisting or not, lets you do as you will;
With bathing and feeding, the long day to fill.
Is that what you're thinking, is that what you see?
Then open your eyes nurse, you're not looking at me.

I'll tell you who I am, as I sit here so still,
As I move at your bidding, as I eat at your will.
I'm a small child of ten . . . with a father and mother,
And brothers and sisters who love one another.

A girl of sixteen, with wings on her feet;
Dreaming that soon, a lover she'll meet.
A bride soon at twenty . . . my heart gives a leap;
Remembering the vows that I promised to keep.

At twenty-five, I have young of my own,
Who need me to build a secure and happy home.
A woman of thirty, my young now grow fast,
Bound together with ties that forever should last.

At forty, my young ones have grown up and gone;
But my man is beside me to see I don't mourn.

At fifty, once more . . . babies play 'round my knees;
Again we know children, my loved ones and me.

Dark days are upon me, my husband is dead . . .
I look at the future, I shudder with dread;
For my young are all rearing, young of their own,
And I think of the years and the love I have known.

I am an old woman now, nature is cruel,
'Tis her jest to make old age look like a fool.
The body, it crumbles, grace and vigor depart,
There is now a stone where I once had a heart.

But inside this old carcass, a young girl still dwells,
And now and again my battered heart swells.
I remember the joys, I remember the pain,
And I'm loving and living life over again.

I think of the years . . . all too few, gone too fast,
And accept the stark fact that nothing can last.
So open your eyes nurses, open and see . . .
Not a "Crabbit Old Woman," look closer . . . see "Me."

"Oh, I imagine it's [religion/spirituality] a factor in caregiving. Our faith has always been our guide. We were raised that way. I don't know ~ we probably would have done caregiving anyway [without religion or spirituality] ~ maybe not. I would say it [faith] was important."

Chapter 8

Religion or Spirituality

Chapter Goal: To help caregivers understand the necessity of a strong religious faith or spirituality that promotes an atmosphere of fairness, determination, and personal growth along with a successful caregiving experience.

"Do onto others as you would have them do onto you."
Reciprocity [pay-back] was promoted by the above sentence from the Bible. Reciprocity was a big motivator for all the couples. The overwhelming majority (29 out of 30) of people interviewed agreed that religious or spiritual beliefs helped them cope with their caregiving experiences. Religious beliefs and inner spirituality were discussed in different parts of the interviews which indicated that these two factors had a positive affect on many areas of the caregiving experience. However, the study I did showed that religion and/or spirituality may have had more of an effect on motivation and relationships than on roles played, tasks done, or personality changes.

Some couples were confused about how to answer the question concerning the affect religion or spirituality had on their caregiving. One wife clarified this confusion by stating, "It wasn't any organized religion. We never called a minister for help in this process. It was more in our personal faith and our faith in each other; we would work this out. We would have called a minister for the folks if we had thought it would help them, but nothing like that was done." Other couples expressed this same sentiment.

The following dialogues and narratives will give the reader some insight into how these couples felt about **religion, spirituality,** and **moral reasoning.**

Religion was discussed briefly by some couples and in depth by others. I asked a couple if their religious beliefs **motivated** them in any way. This couple did not agree in their answers.

Wife: "I suppose in the long run it played a part, probably."

Husband: "No, I don't think so."

Question: "Religion made no difference?"

Husband: "Not for me anyway."

Later, when this couple filled out their questionnaire, the husband circled agree to the question on religion helping him to cope with caregiving. I assumed he felt it just didn't motivated him.

When asked if their **religion or spirituality** had **strengthened** them during the caregiving, one wife quickly replied, "Strengthened? It strengthens your faith." Her husband added, "It sure didn't get any less." The wife concluded, "Anytime you have to deal with any problem, it strengthens your faith." (I'm not sure if the word "faith" pertained to religion or spirituality; maybe it pertained to both.)

I asked a retired couple if they found their **religion/spirituality** beneficial in **promoting good relationships** with others involved in the caregiving they had done. The wife's reply was unusual: "Where else do you go, when there is nowhere else to go?" I then asked, "Are you saying you had some religious counseling?" She replied, "No, not necessarily, but it's always nice to know there is somewhere to go, when there is nowhere else to go."

I think this wife was saying that when a situation can no longer be controlled by humans and their technology, then the only place left to go with your problems is to a higher power or church. She may also have been referring to her own inner spirituality with her answers.

One wife attributed the couple's **motivation** for doing the caregiving to their **religious background.** "I would have felt very unchristian-like if I had not taken care of my parents for as long as I could. I think it's a lot on how we [spouses] were brought up. We were both raised in very similar backgrounds. Our families were very close. We were both raised with a very Christian background. So, spiritually, we came from the same page. I never had to probe him, and he didn't have to probe me to keep motivated." (This wife combined their religious faith, which was the same, and their spirituality as key motivators in doing caregiving.)

The same wife, later in the interview, continued stressing the importance of how children are raised. "I think caregiving has a lot to do with how we were raised. I think that people who don't have the benefit of **religious training** would have a little harder time with some of this [caregiving situations]. A lot of it [caregiving] is no fun."

I told a retired couple that **religion** sometimes **motivates** people. Then I asked, "Was that a big factor in your caregiving?"

Wife: "I just felt that I didn't have a choice in doing the caregiving but religion has helped me to make that choice. It wasn't because of the religion that I took care of my parents."

Question: "Was there anything in your religious background that put you into certain roles during the caregiving years?" (I was wondering if religion had taught them male and female roles.)

Wife: "My family went to church all the time. Dad didn't because he passed out in church toward the end [laughs]. He got so he didn't want to go. Mother was a faithful churchgoer. It's [church going] just been a part of my life since the beginning, and I don't know if it's changed any. It [religion] might have become stronger ~ I don't know. He [husband] might have a different story."

Husband: "My dad didn't go to church either, so I can't say it [religion] had anything to do with it [caregiving]."

Wife: "In my case I did a lot of praying. Now, lately, we sold their [elders] house, and everything turned out so wonderfully. The spiritual guidance helped."

This couple definitely **thought of religion as church going**. The husband admitted during the interview that he didn't go to church much. I think this couple used a great deal of inner spirituality but did not know how to express it.

I asked a working couple to expand on some statements they had made about **religion or faith** earlier in the interview. The husband explained, "Scripture states basically that you *'Honor you Mother and your Father.'* Part of that is to give them honor through the name and position they gave you and by being the kind of person they need ~ supportive." His wife summarized their feelings: "I guess you actually go away [when caregiving is completed] feeling that you've done what the Lord wants you to do, and there are blessings in that." (This couple had a very good understanding of what it was like to have **religion and faith.**)

When a younger couple was asked if their **religion or spirituality** was involved in the **decision** to take care of their parents, the husband slowly responded, "I don't think it was." His wife agreed, "Not a big factor." Later in the interview, when the couple was asked if their religion or spirituality helped with family relationships, the husband's answer was similar to his previous answer: "No, I wouldn't say so." However, his wife discussed her religion in some detail: "Maybe a little. I was basically a very religious person. When my mom died, I kind of lost it [religion] for a while. I was really angry but gradually it [religion] came back. I helped my dad go to church sometimes, and I even took my father-in-law to church. It [going to church] helped. It [religion] was always there but until I really needed it, the religion didn't surface."

I told a very talkative couple that I liked to discuss **religious beliefs** and **spirituality** during the interviews. "Do your beliefs help you with the caregiving? Does religion or spirituality motivate you?" The wife smiled and responded, "Oh, I think so. Prayer never hurts anybody." Her husband agreed with her. (This wife went on to explain how she had been brought up going to church. It sounded like she was brought up in a very strict, religious home.)

After discussing **religion and spirituality** in different parts of the interview, I asked a farm couple, "Do you think religion or spirituality had anything to do with motivating you to do caregiving?" The husband thoughtfully replied, "No more than it motivates your daily life." His wife agreed with his answer. I clarified their answers: "I heard you folks say throughout the interview that religion is just part of your life and this experience is just part of your **lifecycle.** So the two work together?" The wife quickly answered, "Right!" Her husband nodded yes

I asked a couple if **religion** had anything to do with the outstanding **moral reasoning** they used to keep good relationships going in their family during the caregiving years?

Wife: "I definitely feel that it did ~ yes."

Husband: "Same with me. I still take Mother to church. We go over to the nursing home and push her in the wheel chair to church."

Question: "During the fifteen years you had to do all this caregiving, do you think your **religion was strengthened,** or did it decrease, or did it stay about the same?"

Wife: "I think it was strengthened. When you go through so many things, you get stronger. I really feel it [religion] has been strengthened."

Her husband agreed with her.

Spirituality was a key factor for one of the elders, according to his caregiving daughter-in-law. "He [father-in-law] enjoyed people. If he got mad ~ look out ~ but he very seldom got angry. He read the Bible sometimes. He never went to church, but he was a believer ~ he was spiritual." (This daughter-in-law also gave her father-in-law credit for helping the couple learn to appreciate life and live each day to the fullest.)

When I asked a couple who had dealt with a difficult mother for many years if their **spirituality or religion** had helped them with this relationship, their answers included both religion and spirituality.

Husband: "I'm sure it helped."

Wife: "Oh, yes!"

Husband: "My mother was religious. She went to church all of the time. I was brought up in a religious home."

Question: "How religious was your mother?"

Husband: "Well, I don't know if I like the word religious." [He gropes to explain.]

Question: "Spiritual?"

Husband: "Yeah."

Question: "Did you rely on your spirituality? [No answer] Did you ever visit with a pastor about your caregiving concerns?"

Husband: "No. I think our pastor knew what was going on."

Wife: "They [church people] knew what was going on. They [church people] supported us ~ probably more than we realized."

I think this couple had used their inner spirituality many times to cope with the demanding mother they took care of for many years. They also had a strong religious background and wonderful faith in themselves and each other.

At the end of one interview I asked a couple, "During all these caregiving experiences, was your **religion or spirituality reinforced** ~ did it get more or less?"

Wife: "Oh, I don't know. I think it stayed about the same."

Husband: "It's [circumstances] the way life is. You're born, you live, you die. None of us are going to get out of it alive."

This husband seemed to be saying that religion and spirituality don't affect life much because life has a certain cycle for everyone, and there is nothing anyone can do about things like death ~ even if a person is religious or spiritual. His wife followed his statement by telling about her father-in-law's death. The husband joined her, and both talked about the events that led to the death of their father. Both spouses showed a great deal of emotion and sadness as they told their story. I think the son had not gotten through the grieving process concerning his father's death because he was very melancholy when he spoke about his relationship with his dad and also the death of his dad. The husband seemed to be expressing a feeling of helplessness when he stated that everyone dies no matter how spiritual they are. However, I do think he realized that religion and spirituality helped make death easier. His expressions not only showed helplessness concerning his dad's situation, but he also expressed acceptance and contentment concerning his own mortality.

A farm couple was asked if their **religion or spirituality** helped motivate them to do caregiving. Their answers were enlightening.

Husband: "I think so. If the spirituality wasn't behind it [caregiving], you would probably think, *'Well, the heck with it [caregiving].'* I don't know. You might think that you don't want to take on this responsibility."

Wife: "I don't know. I suppose it's [spirituality] there. Whatever you do is by the grace of God. If you don't have God in your life, you are not going to do these things [caregiving tasks]. I don't know. I don't think that [religion] motivated me to do it." The wife then turned and looked at her husband. "I loved your folks ~ I did." (The wife showed a great deal of emotion at this point in the interview.)

Question: "Then your key motivation was the affection you felt for your in-laws?"

Wife: "Right! Right!"

Love was the key motivation for this wife, but she may have gotten that ability to love and care about people because of her **inner spirituality**. I asked this same couple if spirituality was a factor in their family relationships being so good during the caregiving.

Husband: "Oh, no. I think we just kept plugging away."

Wife: "This [caregiving] is part of living."

Husband: "It was the right thing to do."

Wife: "Our parents would of helped us if we were in that situation."

Husband: "Yeah."

Question: "So, another big factor in your caregiving was reciprocity. You helped them because they had helped you in the past?" [Both nodded, yes.]

Wife: "We wanted to do the caregiving. It was hard, but we wanted to."

This couple's spirituality included loving, caring, and reciprocating. I thought they were very spiritual, but they didn't realize it. They were also very humble as were most of the couples I interviewed. It was very difficult for any of these people to talk about themselves and their spirituality. Maybe they felt they would be bragging if they said they had good spirituality.

One couple talked about their **personal faith and inner spirituality** when they were asked about how religious faith and spirituality motivated them to do caregiving. The wife began the discussion: "Yes, this [belief in Christ] has been our life. Christ comes first in my life. What He [Christ] did for us, we need to do for others." This wife then went on in depth to explain how she felt about Christ. The wife seemed to have a deep inner spirituality that she wanted to share with me. After the wife finished her confession, I asked the husband how he felt about spirituality. He answered, "Oh yeah. I guess so." This indicated to me that he agreed with his wife and had the same inner spiritual faith she did but did not want to confess it openly to me. He was also showing a great deal of emotion at this time and seemed to want to end the discussion.

Moral reasoning was a difficult topic to discuss. Many couples did not understand what I meant by moral reasoning. I asked one couple, "You keep saying that caregiving was the right thing to do. This is a type of **moral reasoning**. Did this experience change your moral reasoning in any way?"

Husband: "I don't think it [moral reasoning] changed. I think it was good before and is still good like it always was."

Question: "So, maybe moral reasoning was reinforced?"

Wife: "Yes, that's what I would say. It [moral reasoning] was reinforced. Moral reasoning made us feel that we always thought caregiving was the right thing to do, and now, we know it was the right thing to do because we have done it, and we feel good about having done it. I'd have a hard time now if I hadn't done all the things I did for our parents. Some of the things [nursing help] I did for my husband's mother were pretty rough. I have no regrets. Moral reasoning just reinforced what you thought you should be doing, so you did the caregiving, and now, you are happy."

When a farm couple was asked if they used their **faith** to help them through any **conflicts or stressful times**, they talked about getting help with **decision making.**

Wife: "Oh, yes. It [faith] helped. You had somebody else to talk to. You had someone else to help make decisions." (She was referring to people at her church.)

Question: "Did you go to a pastor or someone to help you at times?"

Husband: "Oh yeah. You look into the word of God to find support; then, you do what you should do."

This couple seemed to be saying that good decisions were made by using moral reasoning supported by the word of God.

I asked another couple if their moral reasoning had changed any during the caregiving years. The wife seemed to be uncertain of her answer until the husband answered.

Husband: "I don't think so. No. I don't know."

Wife: "I don't think so."

Husband: "I just had it in the back of my mind to help anybody any way I could, and it just happened to be my parents that needed help."

Question: "The idea of caregiving for others was always with you from your childhood and continued throughout your life?"

Both spouses agreed to my question with a yes nod of their heads. This couple didn't realize that they had been taught **good moral reasoning** from their childhood. The idea of caregiving for anyone that needed help was so embedded in their thinking that they didn't think of it as a form of good moral reasoning.

Summation

It was evident from the interviews and the questionnaire answers that the vast majority (97%) of the individuals used some form of religion or spirituality to help them get motivated and cope with the caregiving experience. I believe that all of the individuals interviewed had inner spirituality from the way they talked and their expressed need to help their parents. Decisions were made with **common sense** promoted by **good moral reasoning,** which these adults had learned through the religious training they had received in their childhoods. Strong religious beliefs or spirituality did promote successful caregiving.

Chapter Chuckle:

You know you are getting old when . . .

- You are 17 around the neck, 42 around the waist, and 90 around the golf course.
- You are cautioned to slow down by your doctor instead of by the police.
- You have everything you had 20 years ago, only it's all a little bit lower.

"I think you can wait too long to put people [elders] into nursing homes, and then, they don't adapt to the home. They [elders] have to go into the homes while it [staying at the home] can still be a positive experience."

Chapter 9

Institutionalization

Chapter Goals: To help caregivers understand how to put elders into nursing homes, why or when to put elders into homes, what feelings are involved when putting elders into nursing homes, and how to use this extended care service for a successful caregiving experience.

"We didn't want to put them into a home, but . . ."

Most of the couples wanted to keep their parents out of nursing homes as long as possible; therefore, most elders were not put into homes until they needed intensive care for severe mental or physical conditions. In my study, thirty-two elders [17 females and 15 males] were in nursing home care for periods of several weeks to periods of several years.

In a 1997 journal article, "Institutionalization: A continuation of Family Care," Donald Stull, Janet Cosbey, Karen Bowman, and William McNutt proposed that families do not abandon their elders after institutionalization. This was certainly true of the twelve couples who used nursing home services. These couples continued visits with elders, provided outings for elders, and helped with any services the nursing home required of them. Stull and his associates suggested that adult children experience a significant amount of guilt, depression, or anxiety when they put parents into nursing homes. This was not true of the majority of couples in my study, who put parents into homes. Stull's study also suggests that there is no difference in caregiver well-being after care recipients are institutionalized. This seemed to be true for the caregivers in my study.

The degree of care and type of care may change after institutionalization. Involvement by caregivers in personal care such as bathing, eating, dressing, toileting, and clothing care is often reduced but not totally eliminated. In most cases, help with the care of the elder's legal and financial matters continues unchanged after institutionalization. After elders are put into nursing homes, new issues and stressors may arise because of scheduling, problems with the nursing home staff, efforts made by the adult children to be advocates for their elders, and the declining health of the elder.

The dialogue and narrative in this chapter will be divided into four categories:

- How elders were put into nursing homes
- Why or when couples put elders into nursing homes
- How couples felt when they put elders into nursing homes
- What the couples thought about the nursing homes they put their parents into

Each category should give the reader insight into the process the couples went through concerning nursing home care for their parents.

How elders were put into nursing homes

As mentioned earlier in the book, one son told how his family had done an intervention with all siblings present to start the process of putting their parents into a nursing home. The conversation started when the son was asked how his siblings helped him with the caregiving.

Husband: "One example was this fall when we [couple] decided to go see the local nursing homes because we didn't feel Mom and Dad could be out at the farm for another winter. We checked for openings. One home had an opening. So, I called my siblings. They said, *'We've been thinking about that; we agree 100 percent.'* Two days later, they came after dinner and we went to see the folks."

Wife: "They all did an intervention."

Husband: "All three of us went up to the folks' house. Mom and Dad knew something was up when they saw us coming."

Wife: "The three siblings all supported each other because it was hard for all three of them."

Husband: "They [siblings] had no qualms about putting Mom and Dad into basic care. They were very understanding."

Question: "Did your parents help make the final decision when it was presented?"

Husband: "When we first mentioned it to them, we started the conversation with, *'Mom, we don't think you and Dad can be out here this winter. We need to make some arrangements, and it's not too soon to start.'* The key phrase was not *'now is the time, but because winter is coming.'* Right away Dad was very agreeable."

Wife: "Well, your dad decided he needed to be in a nursing home."

Husband: "He didn't think he could be in basic care. Then, Mom said to him, *'Well, you don't need to be in a home,'* so we kind of just left it at that. A couple days later Mom said, *'Well, if we can get Dad someplace, I can live out here [on the farm].'* We left it alone and didn't push it. Later, when we were combining, my siblings and Mom and Dad went to town and they found an opening in a basic care home. To be in a basic care home, you have to be able to take care of yourself and move around. Dad couldn't do that because he needed help walking; however, Mom was able to take care of herself and help Dad. When they got home, Mom said, *'Well, we can't go there.'* So we waited some more."

Wife: "We were afraid if we waited too long, we'd lose that spot. We just had to be persistent."

Husband: "I remember a couple days later I was at the folks' house and I said, *'Mom, have you thought any more about this nursing home?'* She said, *'Well, I can stay out here, and maybe Dad can go to the home; I don't know if I can take care of Dad much longer.'* I just said, *'Mom, you can't stay out here by yourself.'* She looked at me and said, *'I know I can't.'* From that point on, she was talking about going into the home, but she had too many things to do before she could go. We took it upon ourselves to get everything lined up to move into the nursing home, and when the day came to move, she was ready."

Wife: "She was kind of going through the stages of grief. We all go through that in our own way." (Losing her home was a grieving process for the mother.)

Husband: "They [elders] were really accepting the fact [moving to the basic care nursing home] at the end. They had two rooms, and they could bring their own furniture. They were moving to a different place, but it was as much like home as we could make it. They were ready to move then ~ that day. Lots of family members were there to help with the move. It would have been very hard if they had said, *'I don't want to go'* after we had everything ready."

Question: "What I'm hearing you say is that you were very patient, used lots of tact, had family cooperation, were persistent, and at the end you had to be firm. Is that correct?"

Husband: "Yup!"

In my opinion, this family did all the procedures involved correctly when elders need to be put into some kind of professional care facility, especially if the elders were not too agreeable about being put into such facilities. Letting the elders think about each suggestion family members made and letting the elders help make the final decision were brilliant strategies needed to make the nursing home move a success.

Another couple told about a mother they had put into a nursing home who did not want to go into the home.

Husband: "She [mother] did not want to go."

Wife: "My husband's sister was here, and we all talked about putting Mother into a home. She's [the sister] the one that make the final decision. I didn't have to make that decision. Our sister talked to Mother's doctor, and the doctor agreed." (The wife seemed to be happy she hadn't made the decision.)

A working wife explained how her father-in-law decided to go into a nursing home. "We had talked it over with Gramps; he was ~ like I say ~ alert until the end. I had put him on the nursing home list, and they had called us once in June and said they had an opening, but I said, *'I don't think Gramps is ready to go yet.'* Then, they called at the end of July and said they had another opening, and he could have a private room. My husband made me talk to Grandpa, [both laugh] so I said, *'What do you think Gramps, it's the end of July, and fall will be coming soon. They might not have another room ~ the snow will be here soon ~ do you think we should take it? We can come and bring you home for weekends or a day now and then.'* He said, *'Yeah, maybe we should.'"*

Question: "He helped make the decision?"

Wife: "Definitely, definitely!" (It was a very good strategy to let the elder help make the decision.)

One couple told of how their elderly mother and a sibling made the decision for the mother to go into a nursing home.

Wife: "We got to a point at one time where we were going to move Mom in with us. The Lord seemed to intercede for us on that because at the same time we were getting ready to have her move in here [the couples home], a room opened up at a nursing home. My husband's brother was here, and he took her [elder] out for a ride and discussed this move with Mom. Mom made the decision to go into the nursing home herself. We didn't have to say, *'Put her there'* or talk her into going. She, along with her other son, prayed about it and made the decision herself. It took a big burden off of us at that point in time."

Another couple explained in detail how their elders had been put into nursing homes.

Wife: "We basically made the decision on our own, and they [elders] kind of decided to go, too. Except for my mother, we had to put her into a home ourselves because she didn't know what was going on. (The Mother had Alzheimer disease.) When my husband's Dad had a stroke, and his mother couldn't take care of him [the Dad], she put him into a nursing home. When my husband's mother had a stroke, she made her own decision; she said she would go into a home because she knew she couldn't take care of herself anymore. She even asked the nursing home managers to let her know when they had an opening while she was still in the hospital. That's the hard part ~ if you have to make that decision and tell them [elders] they have to go into a nursing home, and they don't want to. That's the very hard part to do. His [husband's] dad didn't want to go, but he had to."

Question: [to the husband] "How did you handle that when your dad didn't want to go into a home?"

Husband: "He was in the condition where he was completely dependent on someone else taking care of him. It was hard to do, but he didn't have much other choice. When he [father] was in the home, Mother was still active, and she had an apartment close by the nursing home, so she was there every day. When he got so she could take him over to the apartment, she took him over to her apartment every day. Mother pretty much had the responsibility at that time ~ trying to handle him when they were at the apartment; it wasn't very easy."

Wife: "And for my dad ~ he knew he couldn't take care of himself anymore. He had a collapsed lung, and he knew he couldn't take care of himself. We told him he could come and we'd take care of him, but as old as he was, he didn't want to be that dependent on his kids. He wanted to go into the nursing home. It was his decision. It's still hard to have them go in there [nursing homes] even if they agree to it." (The wife was very emotional at this point.)

This couple's elders helped make the decisions about going into the home, but it was still very sad for the couple to see their parents go into the homes and realize that there wasn't any way that they could continue to take care of their parents.

A very talkative wife explained how her mother was put into a nursing home. "I talked to the trained nurse that came and checked mother's vital signs before she went into a nursing home. I said, *'I think Mom's getting awfully depressed; she cries a lot.'* When she [the nurse] came, other than to do the vital signs, she quizzed Mom, and Mom started to cry so the nurse said she needed an antidepressant. I took Mom to the clinic. The doctor said, *'You've got her name on a waiting list?'* I said that I never put her name on a waiting list because I didn't think it would go this fast. And then he said, *'I told you six months ago to put her name on a waiting list.'* Well, then he said it was time. She wanted to go. She said she forgot things every day and just couldn't handle things anymore. After the doctor said, *'You've got her on a waiting list?'* And I said, *'Well, no, we didn't,'* he [doctor] said she had to go right now. So I just drove down 281 from Carrington to Jamestown and talked to the guy [a nursing home manager] and said my mom needs to go on a waiting list. He said she can come in on Tuesday. So, there wasn't even time to think. In the back of your mind, you can see it coming, and I just felt I had done it [caregiving] as long as I could, and my brother had done it as long as he could, and she [mom] wanted to go. It gets to the point where you don't feel you are adequate, and I figured they're [professional caregivers] going to do a lot better job than I did. So, I have no regrets."

This explanation was one of the longest I heard but very clearly explained what these couples went through to put their parents into nursing homes. They waited until there were no other alternatives available, and many times a doctor had to say, *'The time has come; do it!'* before they made the move. Some couples were in denial as to how frail their parents were. It took professionals to get them to understand that their elders needed intensive care.

Why or when couples put elders into nursing homes

The two reasons most couples put elders into nursing homes were because *they could no longer perform the intensive medical care the elders needed and the mental stress caregiving caused became overwhelming.* Most couples put elders into the nursing homes as a last resort, when there were no other avenues the couple could pursue to help them with the caregiving.

When I asked a farm couple why they put their elders into a

nursing home, the husband answered, "My dad has to be there because physically he can't be home. He needs someone to help him walk and with other medical treatments. My mom really doesn't physically have to be in basic care, but she likes it there because she gets help with Dad, and there is always something to do. She gets up early, gets dressed, and gets her hair combed because they [elders] have to go to breakfast. At 10:00 a.m. there might be church ~ she goes to whatever church there is ~ then, it's dinner. In the afternoon from 2:00 to 3:00 p.m., there is always some activity, and then there is coffee."

Wife: "They get lots of company."

Husband: "Lots of company and then they are ready to go to supper. When Mom was home, there was no one but her and Dad all day. If you popped in there at 3:00 p.m., Mom still had her old cloths on; she wouldn't put on any makeup, she was sitting in the chair, and she looked like a very old lady. But now whenever you go to the home, she's got a little lipstick on, her hair is combed, and she's got a nice blouse on . . ."

Wife: "It's been a positive change."

This couple was trying to say that the caregiving the elderly mother was doing for their father was taking its toll on their mother. At the nursing home where she got some help, she had some time to take care of herself and do some activities she was interested in. The nursing home facilities were good for both parents.

After telling me how their elder was put into a nursing home, a husband told me why the elder needed to be in the home.

Husband: "We just couldn't keep her here anymore because we are both working; besides that, she couldn't get up and down the steps." (Their house had lots of steps.)

Wife: "I just don't think I could have handled it anymore. (This wife had taken care of three other elderly parents until they died.) I have health problems of my own. I have a bad back."

Many couples as they aged found it more and more difficult to take care of a frail elder because they were needing some care themselves.

Another husband explained why he had to put his mother into a nursing home. "The last year at home was bad, but she didn't want to go to the nursing home until she finally had to. It got so bad we had to go into town at times to help her go to the bathroom. We knew there would be somebody at the nursing home to take care of her at all time."

I reminded a couple about an earlier statement, "You did mention earlier that your dad ended up in a nursing home for a bit."

Husband: "About two months."

Question: [to the wife] "Did your dad ever end up in a home?"

Wife: "No, my dad died in the hospital."

Question: [to the husband] "That must have been a good feeling for you when he [husband's father] didn't have to spend a whole lot of time in the nursing home?"

Husband: "At last there, we kind of had to put him into a home. It was a necessity. He couldn't get around. Without being able to walk, somebody would of had to stay with him all the time."

A retired couple tried to explain why they had put their mother into a nursing home.

Husband: "We tried to take care of her in her own apartment, but we couldn't because she had to be put in and out of bed. She was sick part of the time. She used a walker all the time."

Wife: "She had surgery done at the time."

Question: "So the reason she went to the home was because physically she couldn't get around?"

Husband: "Right. She knew that was it."

Wife: (Told about an incident that scared the mother and then she decided to go into the home.) "That did it. She [elder] knew she couldn't take care of herself anymore. So, she decided to go into the nursing home." (The mother made this decision herself, so it was easier for the couple to accept.)

A son tried to explain why his mother went into a nursing home. "It kind of went along with her independence ~ she felt if she lived with us, she would be a burden. We had a room all fixed up for her. I think one of the things that helped her make that decision [to go into a nursing home] is that she felt if she lived with us she'd be a burden on us. We had everything fixed so she wouldn't. But when given the option, this was the option she took [going into the nursing home]."

Question: "You mentioned earlier that your mother had the start of Alzheimer's disease. She was obviously still clear enough of mind to make that decision to go into a home?"

Husband: "Yes."

Wife: "After she went into the home, she had surgery and things went downhill from there. Her Alzheimer's got worse. She just needed too much care. There would be no way a person could do it on your own. I think that if you did, you'd ruin your own health."

This elderly mother was very independent and didn't want to be a burden to her children, so even with her mental condition getting worse, she was determined to be independent.

An older couple talked about the time they put their mother into a home. I asked, "How did you decide when the time was right? What were some of the clues?"

Wife: "I guess it was because she was down in the hospital . . ."

Husband: "And it was the pneumonia thing."

Wife: "The pneumonia."

Husband: "She was getting harder to handle."

Wife: "At the time that she went into the home she was still on some kind of a machine, some kind of a breathing machine, so we just didn't know if we could handle all that around here; so, that was the right time."

One husband explained why the couple had put their parents into a nursing home. "My wife's mother has so many medications; both of her parents use so many medications. Now that they are in a nursing home, the nurses come in and take blood tests all the time. They [elders] need to be checked almost every day. My wife used to haul her parents to the doctors in Devils Lake many times a month. Her parents also needed medication for all the pain they had. My dad had Alzheimer's disease and needed to have someone with him at all times because it wasn't safe to leave him at home alone." The son then told of several incidents where the father almost killed himself with some of the things he did.

Another son explained why elders had to be put into nursing homes. "As long as they were able to take care of themselves or needed a little assistance, we could take care of them, but when it came to where they needed full-time nursing care, then the nursing homes were a good place for them to be. I mean, nobody likes to put their parents into homes. Most of them [elders] don't want to be there too bad, but when they need 24 hour care, you don't have a whole lot of other choices."

A retired couple gave me some reasons why their parents were put into nursing homes.

Wife: "She [mother] had a compressed fracture in her back, so she couldn't walk. So, her options were to come and live with one of us [siblings] or go to the nursing home. There were no other options. If you can't walk, you can't take care of yourself. I thought at the beginning ~ if that ever healed ~ but you know at 90, they [professionals] couldn't do much for her. If she'd gotten better, she could have come home, but she just got worse."

Question: "You felt that was a good place for her to be at that point?"

Wife: "It was the only place. Where else would you go?" (I think the wife was becoming a bit irritated with me at this point.)

Question: [to the husband] "How about your dad. Did he end up in the nursing home?"

Husband: "Yes, he wasn't there very long. He finally went in when he couldn't walk anymore. He wasn't there no three months, maybe eight weeks, I don't know, it wasn't very long."

Wife: "He got so he couldn't eat. He was dying when he went into the nursing home."

Husband: "He was having little strokes, I think."

This couple took care of their parents until both elders were very frail and sick. The elders were very independent and wouldn't live with their children. So, the only option, when they became incapacitated, was to go into the nursing homes.

One couple explained why their parents were put into nursing homes. The elders didn't want to go to nursing homes but knew they were at the stage in their lives where they needed intensive care, so they accepted their faith when their adult children and some professionals said it was time to go into a home.

Wife: "She [mother] did not want to be alone. She was afraid of the dark. She was afraid that if she turned something on in the morning she wouldn't remember how to turn it off later in the day. That's how fast it was going [the Mother's deterioration]. One day she opened the garage door and then she called me to come into town because she didn't remember how to shut it. I told her to touch the remote, but she didn't know what the remote was. She knew in the morning, but by night she had forgotten. So, I went to town and closed the garage door."

Question: [to the wife] "Your mother had Alzheimer's disease; what is your dad's problem?"

Wife: "He can't walk from me to you. He's completely wheelchair bound."

Husband: "He's completely worn out."

Wife: "Even his arms ~ we were talking about him last summer ~ his arms can't push himself in his wheelchair. He's so weak he can't stand up or switch himself in the bathroom. He looks like a big man, but he is very frail. I don't know that he could take a step."

Husband: "No, he couldn't take a step. He's just too weak."

Wife: "Thank God they're [elders] in a place where he [father] still has a good mind and he can tell her [mother] things and help her, and she's got a good body and can walk all over the place if she just knew where she was going." [laughs]

Question: "They can still help each other?"

Wife: "Like I said, thank God that the doctor said she should go into the home while she could make the adjustment. If we had waited another few months, I don't think she would have made that adjustment because she couldn't. It's taken a year for her to call it [nursing home] home. Dad went in April, and Mother went in June. Dad would like to be back home, but he knows he can't. His condition is way too frail."

None of the elders were put into nursing homes while they were still in good health; it was only when the care became very extensive that the decisions were made by the adult children, professionals, or the elders themselves to go into nursing homes.

How couples felt when they put elders into nursing homes

The one word expressed most often when couples were asked how they felt when their parents were put into nursing homes was "**relief.**" Here are some examples:

I asked a couple that had talked about trying their best to keep their mother out of the nursing home, "How did you feel when the time came, and you had to put your mother into a home?"

Husband: "Well, I guess for us it was kind of a **sigh of relief,** when she did have to go into the home. There were times when she couldn't even answer the phone herself. We tried calling, and we couldn't get her, so we'd have to get into the car and run into town and check on her."

I asked a couple whose father had only spent two months in a nursing home before he died, "How did you feel when you finally had to put your father into a home?"

Wife: "It really was a **relief.** The day we were going to take him to the home, it was like deja`vu. Gramps had gotten up in the night and fallen. This frightened him and made him think he had made the right decision by deciding to go into a nursing home. After he went into the home, he got gradually worse. He always wanted to come home. I'd say, *'I don't have your car keys here today.'* He'd say, *'Oh, okay.'* So, you could easily talk him out of stuff. But he got worse . . ." (The wife became very emotional and quit talking.)

Question: "He sounds like a very agreeable man to work with?"

Wife: "Yes. He was."

I asked an older couple how they felt after they put their mother into a nursing home. The husband slowly and thoughtfully replied, "Well, I guess in all honesty you feel **relieved** because you're not quite as responsible for her as you were when she was living with you. Like I said earlier, it's [caregiving] kind of a 24 hours a day job, but now we go down to the nursing home two or three times a week to see her, and in my mind I can see that they [nursing home staff] are doing everything that is necessary for her down there." His wife added, "We missed her because we did a lot of different things with her. Now, we spend quite a bit of time down at the home with her." (This couple's mother had lived with them for many years before she went into the nursing home.)

When I asked one couple how they felt when they had to put their parents into a nursing home, the wife quickly answered, "It's a **relief** to know that they [elders] are being taken care of." Her husband echoed this sentiment, **"Relieved**, just relieved. I couldn't keep on like that [taking care of a father with Alzheimer's] and neither could my sister. He [elder] needed special care."

A wife explained with a great deal of emotional sadness how it feels when you put your parents into a nursing home: "The deal of putting them in the nursing home ~ it's just like you've gone through a funeral, but you know you're going to have to go through it [a funeral] again in a few years. That's just the feeling you have at first when you put them [elders] into a home. That's how bad you feel about it, and then you know you're going to have to go through that [funeral] again ~ yourself ~ if you live long enough. That's the hard part of putting them into a nursing home." Her husband agreed with his wife's feelings with an emotional "yes."

Another couple expressed how good it made them feel when the elders enjoyed being in the nursing home and were doing much better since they had been put there.

Husband: "Dad looks better since he's in the nursing home."

Wife: "Yes he does."

Husband: "At home he'd worry that the water softener was leaking or that the car was leaking oil, now he doesn't worry about any of that."

Wife: "It just reaffirms our feelings that they needed help."

Husband: "We did the right thing."

Wife: "We feel good about that."

Husband: "If you'd go there [nursing home], and they'd say, *'God, I want to get out of here,'* you'd feel terrible. But it feels good to go there and see that they are happy."

Wife: "Seeing them look more like themselves again makes us happy."

Husband: "They look better."

Wife: "That was a case where my husband and I saw them [elders] change more than the two other siblings saw them change because they'd [siblings] only see them [elders] on special occasions. Our parents would be fired up then [on special occasions] and get the makeup on, but we'd see them day to day. Mother has always been a very social person. She'd go to all the activities and do things. She didn't do anything anymore. She didn't bake or put makeup on. She didn't do house cleaning. To see this change in Mother was as much of a change as in Dad [the father was very sick physically]. Now that they are in the nursing home, seeing them more like themselves makes us think we did the right thing."

A working couple was asked how they felt now that their mother was in a nursing home. The wife quickly answered, "I really feel good about it now; she's [elder] better about it [this elder did not want to go to the nursing home at first]. I know there are times she's [elder] lonely. We explain to her that we are very tired when we get home from our work. There are two other sets of married kids living close by that can go visit her, too." Her husband added, "They [other kids] go to see her [elder], too." (It seemed to me that the husband would have liked to have taken care of his mother longer than he had but he also realized his wife was getting older and with her full-time job could not handle all the elder caregiving tasks required for his frail mother.)

Another son told me how he felt when he put his mother into a nursing home: "Well, we couldn't do what they [nursing staff] are doing for her in the home. It would just be impossible for us to give her the kind of care she needs right now. I think we're doing the best we can." This son had no guilt about putting his mother into the home because she was getting better care than he and his wife could give her; however, he did mention during the interview that he felt guilty when he did not go and visit his mother in the home every day because he lived close to the nursing home.

Feelings were difficult for the couples to express and some couples avoided my questions when I asked them about feeling. They all showed sadness and emotion when they talked about putting their parents into nursing homes. They also felt they had done the best they could for as long as they could, so none of the couples experienced much guilt about putting elders into nursing homes when there were no other options left to pursue.

What the couples thought about the nursing homes

The majority of the couples who had put elders into nursing homes felt the nursing homes did a good job; however, some couples felt there was room for improvement. I asked a couple who had taken care of all four of their parents and had put only one parent into the nursing home for a short time, "Do you feel the nursing home does a good job?"

Wife: "Well, I feel they do a pretty good job. There are a few things they could do a little better. Mother says that sometimes it takes a long time for them to come when she puts her light on. That maybe feels like a very long time to her but not so long for the people that are working there."

Question: "You mean the homes could use more help?"

Wife: "Ah-hum, [nods yes]."

Question: [to the husband] "How about you?"

Husband: "I think they are doing a good job. You can't expect them to be right there all the time. They have to take care of other people, too. Every day is a big adjustment for our mother because she's used to being by herself."

Wife: "She's got a roommate and a small room."

This wife was trying to say that the mother might be unhappy because she now had to share a small space with someone else when she had been used to living alone in her own home. The wife wasn't blaming the home for this condition, she was just stating a fact about nursing homes that makes some elders unhappy when they go into the homes.

Another husband and wife did not totally agree on the services provided by a nursing home. When I asked, "Do you feel the nursing home did a good job?" the husband quickly answered, "Yes." His wife had a different opinion.

Wife: "In a way they do, but I've had some bad experiences with incompetent nurses and aides. My husband's mother had her mind and the things she told me I know happened. I saw some of it happen. I would go down to the front desk and say, *'Hey, stop doing this,'* but it didn't help. They [nursing homes] all say they are short of help. That is no reason to be mean to somebody. My parents were in a nursing home, too, and they were ill treaded, too. It goes on and it's no good. I think it should be mandatory that all nursing homes have cameras in every room and in the hallways, then there would be no ill treatment of patients. If it's [cameras] too costly, then the family should be able to have an option of installing the cameras."

The couple then discussed this proposal between themselves, and the wife concluded, "It may infringe on the nurses rights, but the nurses sometimes infringe on the patents rights, too."

A couple who was very happy with the nursing home care their mother had gotten told of how the mother had checked herself into the home and later checked herself out. The husband commented, "She [elder] was very happy, I thought, when she was in the nursing home. She just loved it there and the people that worked there. She was paying her own way and decided it cost too much; that's the reason she moved out. I'm sure she didn't move because she didn't like it there." This elderly mother went to live with one of her children after she left the home.

A wife expressed an opinion about a nursing home where her mother-in-law was a patient. "I feel good about the nursing home. There are times when I walk into the home and see some things I don't like, and I feel, *'Why does this happen,'* but it's [the nursing home] more positive than it is negative."

An older husband had an opinion about the nursing home his mother was in, and his wife had an opinion about visiting the nursing home.

Husband: "The nursing home my mother is in ~ at this time anyway ~ is a very, very good place for old people because the home has a staff that gets along so well with all the residents, and they [staff] also have many things to do for entertainment in the home. They [staff] do a great job down there, and it takes special people to work in a nursing home. They [staff] have an advantage because they come in and work their shifts; then, they can go home. They do a nice job. I am happy with the nursing home my mother is in." (This husband was saying that it's harder for caregivers to take care of parents 24 hours a day than it is for a nursing home staff because they can get away from the caregiving after eight hours.)

Wife: "One thing ~ like when we go to visit Mother in the nursing home ~ we stop and talk to a lot of people that are in the home. They are so happy to have us stop and visit with them. You feel good when you've done something like that."

When I asked one couple about putting parents into nursing homes, the husband tried to explain that the care continued after the elders were institutionalized. I think he was trying to tell me that they didn't shirk their responsibilities by putting their parents into nursing homes.

Husband: "There's still a lot of work, paper work, when they are in the homes. I'm sure you know that?" (Laughs) I nodded yes. He continued, "I'm thankful for nursing homes. I don't know what we'd have done with Dad. (His father had Alzheimer disease.) We'd of just had to stay with him all the time. Somebody has to take care of people when they can't take care of themselves ~ be bathed ~ in a wheel chair ~ toward the end. I don't know how we would have taken care of him at home."

Wife: "I think that's a really good point. You really appreciate those people in there [nursing home staff]. They take really good care of them [elders]."

Husband: "When you go in there [homes] and see all the people [elders] and what is being done for them, you wonder where would they be and who would be taking care of them if there were no nursing homes."

Question: "Somebody would have to live with them?"

Wife: "You'd have to have two shifts."

This couple was very thankful for nursing homes and felt they did a good job. The couple knew what was involved with elder caregiving because they had done it for many years before they put their parents into homes.

One son, when I was asking a question about insight the couple had gained during their caregiving years, responded, "You know, they [elders] get very, very good care in nursing homes wherever they go in this town [town has more than one home]. Go up there [to the local nursing homes] and spend a little time with them [patients]. If you don't show up, they [patients] are a little disappointed." I guess this son was trying to tell me that he'd learned that the local nursing homes do a very good job of taking care of elders and that it is important to visit elders in nursing homes, even if these elders are not your relatives.

A farm wife, who felt that parents should be put into the nursing homes before they are too mentally disabled, discussed her mother's case with me. "She's been in the home about a year and it has taken her all this time to find her way to her room. If I had waited too long to put her into the home, she could not have made that simple adjustment. When we are there visiting and she says, *'I want to go home,'* she means her room. She has no recollection of her former home. So, I think it's really important for Alzheimer's patients that the doctor knew enough to get her into the home before she was too bad. Now that [nursing home] is home, and she can find her way to the bathroom and her room, but she can't get to Dad's room. She only has to learn about three things in there ~ she's going to make it."

A couple who had put all four parents into a nursing home when they could no longer take care of them was asked, "So, at that point you felt the nursing home was the best place for them?"

Wife: "Yes."

Husband: "We wouldn't of had the room or the facilities here to take care of them."

Wife: "No, we couldn't take care of them anymore."

Husband: "We couldn't take care of them as well as they could at the nursing homes."

Wife: "It's nice to be in a nursing home when you are from that community because when people come in to visit their elderly parents, they visit with others they know. They [patients] sit right by the door, especially on Sunday, waiting for someone to talk to them. It is a good thing that there is a lot of visiting back and forth between people that come to visit their own elders in the home. Some of us people, who came to visit our parents, got to be friends. (Laughs) We would visit with them [people that had elders in the home] all the time, too."

This couple felt that the people who would come to visit their parents became a support group for each other. They could talk about similar problems, and if their elder wasn't capable of visiting, they had other visitors to talk to. When I asked this couple for a final comment, they chose to talk about visiting nursing homes.

Question: "Are there any other comments you'd like to make?"

Wife: "Well, I guess not. Some people say they don't like going into the nursing home. I don't think people should have that opinion."

Husband: "That's not a good attitude."

Wife: "People in the nursing home ~ if they know anything at all ~ like to have people come and visit."

Husband: "Someday if they [people that don't like to go to nursing homes] end up in there [homes] they will like to see company besides just the other residents in the nursing home."

Question: "It's really special if someone besides a son or daughter comes?"

Husband: "Yes, even today, we still stop in at the nursing home once in a while. They [residents in the homes] appreciate that."

This couple still went to visit nursing homes even though all their family members had died. This couple now had a mission in life: to tell others that it was a good idea to visit the nursing homes once in a while because unless a person dies young, most will end up in a nursing home some day.

The majority of the couples that eventually put their parents into nursing homes were very happy with the services performed by the homes. The few complaints about staff members and services were not severe. Spouses often differed in their opinions, so personal perceptions may have varied about similar incidents.

Summation

Although some couples expressed **relief** when elders were put into nursing homes, these couples well-being (quality of life) did not change because the responsibilities of caregiving continued. If an elder didn't want to go to a home, gentle persuasion was used through family interventions. The best method used when putting elders into homes was to let them make the decision to go. Couples put elders into homes when the caregiving became too intense and the couples felt the professionals could do a better job. A great deal of sadness and loss was felt when parents went into nursing homes. However, the nursing homes did a good job of taking care of the elders, so this helped alleviate some of the sadness and loss that occur with institutionalization.

Chapter Chuckle:
You know you are getting older when . . .
- You're sitting in a rocker, and you can't get it started.
- You sink your teeth into a steak, and they stay there.
- You have too much room in your house and not enough in the medicine cabinet.

PART V

IF I HAD MY LIFE TO LIVE OVER AGAIN
By Erma Bombeck

I would talk less and listen more.
I would have invited friends over to dinner even
if the carpet was stained and the sofa faded.
I would have eaten the popcorn in the 'good' living room
and worried much less about the dirt, when someone
wanted to light a fire in the fireplace.

I would have taken the time to listen to my grandfather
ramble about his youth.
I would never have insisted the car windows
be rolled up on a summer day
because my hair had just been teased and sprayed.
I would have burned the pink candle sculpted like a rose
before it melted in storage.

I would have sat on the lawn with my children
and not worried about grass stains.
I would have cried and laughed less while watching television,
and more while watching life.
I would have gone to bed when I was sick, instead of pretending
the earth would go into a holding pattern
if I weren't there for the day.
I would have never bought anything just because it was practical,
wouldn't show soil, or was guaranteed to last a lifetime.

Instead of wishing away nine months of pregnancy,
I'd have cherished every moment and realized that the wonderment
growing inside me was my only chance in life
to assist God in a miracle.

When my kids kissed me impetuously, I would never have said,
"Later . . . now go get washed up for dinner."
There would have been more "I love you's,"
more "I'm sorry's,"
but mostly, given another shot at life,
I would seize every minute . . .
Look at it and really see it and live it . . .
And never give it back.

"It made you feel good ~ knowing you could pay them
[elders] back for all they had done for you."

Chapter 10

Positive Aspects of Caregiving

Chapter Goals: To help future caregivers find answers to their caregiving
dilemmas by understanding the rewards received, lessons learned, and
wisdom acquired when doing successful caregiving.

Is there an answer?
　　I had each person in my survey circle a number from 1 to 10 on a
rating scale to indicate how positive or negative they felt about the
caregiving experience they had. Number 1 was very negative, and number
10 was very positive. All of the 30 individuals that were part of the study
circled a number on the positive end of the scale (6-10). Why was the
caregiving experience so positive for these people? The answer to this
question can be found in the types of **rewards** the caregivers said they
received, the **lessons** they had learned because of the caregiving, and the
advice they wanted to pass along to other caregivers.

Rewards received included
- Feeling good about themselves and what they had done
- Being able to set a good example for their children
- Being appreciated by the elders they took care of
- Being able to share fun activities with their elders
- Having appreciation shown by siblings and community
  members
- Fulfilling spiritual needs
- Gaining in inner strength and personality growth
- Gaining knowledge

　　Feeling good was the reward most cited by all of the couples. One
wife stated, "It gives you a good feeling that you can care for your
parents." This same feeling was expressed in many ways by different

couples. "Knowing you'd done your best" made one couple feel good. Having "peace of mind" made two couples feel good. "Feeling good about having done all that you could do" was expressed by five couples. "Being able to reciprocate" made four couples feel good. Another husband felt an enormous amount of pride in being able to reciprocate. Filling a need to nurture made three wives feel good. One husband summed up this sentiment best: "You feel you've done all you could have done that's the good part. If you hadn't done it, you'd feel bad about it." The **feeling of being needed** was expressed or implied many times when rewards and positive aspects of caregiving were discussed.

Being able to set a good example for children was a primary reward for ten couples. Some couples modeled for their grandchildren. Pride was felt by the couples who had children and grandchildren that helped with the caregiving.

Being appreciated by their elders was another reward that made ten couples feel good. Seeing elders happy and living their final years satisfactorily were rewards for many couples. According to several couples, elders were happy when they were visited in nursing homes and children and grandchildren were brought to see them. The fact that the elder's life may have been extended because of the loving care they had been given made one couple feel good. Three couples expressed pride because they were able to keep their elders out of nursing homes until they died.

Being able to share fun activities with their elders was another positive aspect of caregiving. Five couples mentioned doing crafts, playing bingo, going to church, or going to senior centers as fun activities they shared with their elders. One wife was rewarded by sharing confidences with her mother-in-law. Another wife who had shared many activities with her in-laws announced: "They are fun to take care of." Sharing activities was not only rewarding, but it helped couples grow closer to their elder(s).

Having appreciation shown by siblings and community members was a reward mentioned by five couples. One wife mentioned wanting to continue helping with caregiving in her community after her own parents die because the community has been so complimentary. This same wife had received small financial rewards from a brother on occasions to buy things for herself. Appreciation shown by a sibling and community members made her feel special and gave her the self-esteem she needed to continue with the caregiving.

Fulfilling spiritual needs was very rewarding for four couples. "You've done what the Lord wants you to do, and there are blessings to that," was a comment made by one wife. "That's what we were put on this earth to do ~ to serve other people ~ so, I guess there is spirituality there," was a comment made by a wife when discussing spiritual rewards.

Gaining inner strength and achieving personality growth were rewards expressed by five people in the survey. One wife said, "You maybe gained in inner strength. Sometimes you got frustrated; then you'd say, *'Okay, I can do this. I can balance all this together.'* So, you gained in inner strength."

Gaining knowledge that would help in their own aging was a positive aspect for a majority of the couples. "It was a learning experience, definitely!" was a comment made by a wife and reinforced by many of the couples. Learning about one's own aging and mortality was a substantial reward for a majority of the couples. These couples all felt that caregiving was a challenging and learning experience. Some of the broad areas of caregiving where knowledge was obtained were nursing homes, insurances, power of attorney, professional health care services, Alzheimer's disease, and what it is like to get old. One wife described what she had learned about aging: "I learned that the elderly are helpless. I learned that they are at our mercy. I learned by watching them, what I may have to go through some day. I guess I tried to put myself in their shoes." A husband's opinion on what he had learned was, "I think that you definitely learn what disabilities can get you down. I learned that it's a tough go and you can't do anything for yourself." One wife learned to improve her nursing skills by caregiving. Two couples learned how to appreciate life by taking care of elders who set a good example for them. Two respondents said they'd learned to "be better people." One husband's profound statement about rewards adds a fitting conclusion to positive aspects of caregiving: "Rewards for caregiving come from within. I don't think you can write it down. I don't think it's going to be the same for you, me, or her [his wife]. It's going to have to be something you are going to realize yourself." The **inner feelings** the couples received as rewards for their caregiving were hard to express for many couples.

"What were your rewards?" was a question put to all the caregivers. Many of the answers to this question on **rewards** were similar to responses given in all areas of the interviews. Rewards seemed to blend into answers to many of the questions that were asked. The following quotations and dialogues are some of the respondents answers to my question:

The greatest reward for a farm couple was brought out in the very last statement the wife made: "It's kind of a cycle. If one generation breaks the cycle by not being caregivers ~ it's bad. It's something you pass on to the next generation. The greatest reward is when your children become caregivers."

I asked a very busy couple what some of their rewards for caregiving were. The husband gave me a very good answer: "Satisfaction of being able to be there. I think of what my mom and dad went through to raise us boys during the war, and just to be here for my mom now is a reward. My brother has lost a lot by not being able to be here to take Mom places. I've enjoyed it. We have a great time doing things together, going for rides, teasing her ~ she loves that."

I asked a younger couple, "If you had to make a list of rewards, what would you write?" The husband replied, "I would say the most important thing [reward] for taking care of them [elders] was that we knew what kind of care they were getting. When we put my dad into the nursing home . . . I was concerned about the help. I know they [nursing home staff] are good at what they do, but ~ *'Is he going to fall out of bed and break his neck?'* He was into the falling business. At least when we took care of him, we kind of knew what was going on most of the time."

His wife had a different answer for my question: "You also learned what was important and what could wait [set priorities]. You know the house work is never done, so if I didn't get things done, I thought, *'Well, who's going to know in a hundred years if my house was clean.'* I thought if grandpa is being taken care of, and I'm at his house cleaning, that's where I'm supposed to be." (Caregiving had helped this wife set priorities and be nurturing ~ this was a big reward for her.)

I asked another couple what would be on their list of rewards.

Husband: "It would be very hard to make a list of rewards that are the same for everyone. That's [a list] got to come from each person. I don't think you can write it down. You can't write it down and tell somebody ~ if you do caregiving, there will be rewards."

Question: "What I'm hearing you say is that you have to go through it to realize the rewards that are there?"

Husband: "Right! You have to go through it. You have to do it. I mean ~ it's not going to be the same for two people no matter what you do."

Question: "Would you recommend doing caregiving if it is needed?"

Husband: "Oh, yes."

My question about rewards brought a slow reply from a farmer. "Well, I think it makes a person feel better or feel good, that you did a lot for your parents. I know they [parents] appreciated it, and that makes it [caregiving] a two-way game." (He was talking about feeling good because you gave back and were appreciated for your efforts.) His wife also had an answer: "Peace of mind. I'm glad I did it." Her husband then concluded, "I don't feel we should have done more. I think we did our share, and that's probably about it." (The husband became very emotional and quit talking.)

A farm couple had the following comment to my question on rewards:

Husband: "For me . . . I was taking care of my mom and dad [he showed pride in his body language as he spoke] because they had taken care of me."

Wife: "It gave you a good feeling."

Husband: "Yes, it did. And now I feel good that we did the right thing. They were here [on the farm] as long as they possibly could be. We've lived on this farm together since we were married. We know that if it wouldn't have been for my wife and me, they couldn't have lived here for the last five years. So, we gave them that time, and now they are content. I feel good ~ thinking we did the right thing."

Wife: "I do, too."

Husband: "I don't feel we should of had them moved into basic care two years ago, but I don't think we could of kept them here any longer. I guess I feel we gave them their independence as long as we could, and it turned out pretty good."

The following quote sums it up very well: "It's a good feeling. Sometimes you get disgusted. All in all if I had to do it over again, I would."

Lessons learned included
- How to appreciate life
- If we had to do it again, we would
- Elders really appreciate company when they are in the nursing homes
- Elders get good care in the nursing homes
- How to put elders into nursing homes at the right time
- When to pray for spiritual guidance
- How to network with extended family and community organizations
- How to be sensitive
- The importance of supporting their spouses

"What did you learn?" was asked of all those interviewed.

"You need to be kind and gentle and compassionate. That's what the elderly need. That's what they need to get them motivated. If you don't have compassion and you're grumpy, it just turns their attitude wrong, too. They aren't going to cooperate with you. They [elders] may do the opposite of what you want them to do. It just takes a lot of patience and caring and loving."

This statement made by a wife summed up the responses made by many of the individuals questioned about lessons learned. The following dialogue depicts some of these conversations.

At the end of one interview I said, "Like at the end of every story or fable, there is a lesson to be learned ~ a moral to the story. What is your lesson learned?"

Wife: "What we talked about before ~ it just goes back to appreciating what you have and that you have your health."

Question: "So the lesson you learned was appreciation."

Wife: "Yes, Dad was good natured, and he seemed to enjoy himself all the time. He really enjoyed life ~ was not a complainer ~ it was very seldom that he complained about his legs hurting. He was up and down out of bed a lot. He wasn't on a lot of medication but had some arthritic pain. He set a good example." (I have found this to be true for many elders in their last years of life; they appreciated the life they had lived. Taking care of an elder when they are dying can teach us all how to appreciate what we have and also learn how to die with grace and dignity.)

A valuable lesson concerning their own aging was learned by a farm couple. When I asked them about lessons learned, the husband quickly replied, "If we had to do it again, we would." His wife added, "We pretty much know the operations of the nursing home. [We all laughed] Her husband joined in, "That might not be a good thing." [More laughter] The wife concluded, "I always tell the nurses' aides that when I get there, I'll know what you guys are up to." [Much more laughter]

Another couple learned several important factors about caregiving.

Wife: "Try to boost their [elders] morale, and things will go better for you. Be honest with them [elders]."

Question: [to her husband] "How about you? Were there any lessons you learned?"

Husband: "I don't know. It all happened so fast, and it was over fast."

Wife: "You have to watch for signs ~ dangers to them [elders]."

Husband: "It [Alzheimer's disease] came on so fast."

Question: "You learned some very important things while you were caregiving didn't you?" How to boost an elder's morale, how to be honest, and what Alzheimer's is all about." (Both spouses nodded yes to my statement.)

A thoughtful husband reflected as he made the following statement about what he had learned while caregiving: "Someone once said that it's hard to grow old. People fight it. They like to retain their youth. I guess it's [caregiving] helped me personally, when I see Mom and the process she's going through to grow old more gracefully ~ in a sense." I added, "As we grow older it helps us to realize our own mortality." He agreed.

I asked one couple if they learned anything during their caregiving years that they would like to pass along to others. The husband replied, "I guess if there's a lesson in caregiving, it's just that you better be able to take care of your parents when the time comes. You're going to have to dig in. You maybe even have to let some of your own work go to get stuff done for them."

A younger farm couple had some very precise answers to my question on what they had learned by caregiving.

Wife: "Communication is a big thing. You need good communication with everyone involved in the caregiving."
Husband: "Patience. You need to be patient."
Wife: "Yeah, patience."

Applying the **Golden Rule**, *Do onto others as you would have them do onto you,* was used by one wife and should be a good rule for us all. "If I had anybody taking care of me, I'd want them to be that way with me. (She had talked about being compassionate earlier). I hope I never have to be taken care of. [Laughs] But if I do, that's the one thing I would appreciate." I summed up what we had been talking about: "You learned to follow the **Golden Rule?**" Both spouses agreed to this statement and laughed. I guess they were thinking of how simple it was. All you had to do is follow the **Golden Rule** and everything would work out okay.

Advice given included
- **You will gain knowledge:** "I think everyone needs to participate in that [caregiving] function because you're going to be there one day. Just the time spent learning the insurance procedures and Medicare procedures; that's all knowledge you probably would never have used if you hadn't done that [caregiving]."
- **You will achieve peace of mind:** "I'm glad I did it. I don't know if I'd want my kids to do it for me. I don't know what I'm going to think when I get older. I think peace of mind is what makes you feel good. I'm so glad I did what I did."
- **You will need extended help:** "Have lots of help. . . . Caregivers need to utilize things like respite care offered by hospitals. Everyone needs time off and some time to themselves."

Advice was given in a humble fashion and came straight from the heart. Most of the people interviewed did not feel they knew enough about caregiving to dispense advice to others. One husband, very humbly, said it this way: "I don't think I've got any words of wisdom. Many people take care of their parents for a longer period of time than I did."

It took a great deal of prodding to get any of the couples to give advice, and when they offered advice, it was usually with a sense of humor. An older husband's response to my question concerning **words of wisdom** was, "Be patient. Someday you may be that way, too. If it takes 20 minutes to get into the car ~ start out earlier." [We all laughed.]

Summation

Strategies used, rewards gained, lessons learned, and advice given were all very similar. These areas all involved discussions on communication, networking, patience, understanding, affection, priorities, reciprocity, common sense, attitude, and the **Golden Rule**. The **Golden Rule** is an **attitude** that uses **common sense**. To put it point blank, use some common sense to make caregiving a successful experience.

Chapter Chuckle:

You know you are getting older when . . .

- The best part of your day is over when your alarm clock goes off.
- You get your exercise acting as pallbearer for a friend who exercised.
- "Tying one on" means fastening your Medic-Alert bracelet.

"It wasn't that I had to do it [caregiving], but I chose to do it ~ probably longer than I should have. I have no regrets."

Chapter 11

Making the Decision

Chapter Goal: To convince the reader to do successful caregiving if the opportunity presents itself.

Is that your final answer?

On the TV show, *Who Wants To Be A Millionaire,* the host asks each contestant, "Is that your final answer?" before an answer is accepted from a contestant. This is done to make sure the contestant has thought of all the possibilities before giving a final choice. I ask you to consider all the possibilities, pros and cons, before you make a final choice about caregiving for your parents when the time comes. Let's pretend that you are at the million-dollar question; "Will you help take care of your parents when they become frail elders?" Consider the information I have outlined for you in the preceding chapters and my final review and comments in this chapter before you give me your final answer.

Is there a need?

Current statistics provide evidence that there is an increasing number of aging people in our country. According to a United States Census Bureau Statistical Brief put out in 1995, the elderly population has grown substantially in this century. In 1900, persons over 65 years of age comprised 1 of every 25 Americans, while in 1994, 1 in 8 were over 65. There are two reasons for the increase in the percentage of elders in our population ~ the birth rate is declining and elders are living longer.

Couples are more likely to be taking care of elderly relatives than single persons because of the effect caregiving has on the physical, mental, and social life of the primary caregiver. With the average size of the family decreasing, the one or two adult children in each family will be expected to shoulder all the burdens of caregiving for their parents. Sibling mobility (more children moving long distances from home) will also put the burden of caregiving onto the child that remains closest to the elderly parents. Changing gender roles (women working out of the home) make it important that men take part in the caregiving role.

Why do adult children take care of their elderly parents? There are three theories that give possible answers to this question. One theory suggests that because most children perceive their parents as valuable people and have affection for them, they will want to reciprocate for all the love and caregiving the elders did for them when they were young. A second theory suggests that an elder is part of a family system, so when the needs of the elder change the lives of the adult children will also change to meet these needs. This theory deals with the natural lifecycle process. Adult children take care of their elderly parents, and someday, their children will take care of them. The last theory suggests that as human beings, we have a need for psychological closeness and contact with blood relatives. The psychological bond that was established during childhood will continue throughout the lifecycle for the people that bonded. This bond is emotional; therefore, if the bond is broken before one party dies, there will be emotional repercussions. I believe all three of these theories hold true during the caregiving process and answer the question about what motivates adult children to take care of their elderly parents.

What is the key to successful caregiving?

There are two factors that lay the foundation for successful caregiving.

- *Common Sense:* A form of decision making that is unselfish, understandable, and practical will lead to good attitudes.
- *Good Attitudes:* A readiness to respond favorably to a person, situation, or event is the most important factor for doing successful caregiving.

What was clear to me after I finished my study is that the 15 couples interviewed did not suddenly establish good attitudes toward caregiving when they hit the age of 50 and saw their parents needed help. These people had been raised in communities that took care of their elders. They had been brought up in religious homes where family values were taught on a daily base. They had seen modeling of elder care done by their parents for their grandparents. When it became their turn to take care of their elderly parents, they stepped right up to the base, never once hesitating or asking whether this was the most convenient way to deal with their elder care problem. The couples knew what needed to be done, and they did it.

The key to positive caregiving was using common sense to form and continue using good attitudes. These skills are best learned when we are children. If good attitudes and making common sense decisions are not learned as children, it will be much harder to learn these skills as we age. However, I do feel it is never too late to make changes in our lives. Every healthy, intelligent human being makes their own choices and can control their own actions and behaviors. When a specific way of thinking or acting is not working, a change is needed. As adults we need to raise our children with good attitudes toward elders, especially elders that are relatives. We also need to teach children how to use common sense decision-making, so they grow up doing what is right, not doing what is the most convenient for themselves.

Now, lets briefly review behavior characteristics needed to be successful caregivers. These characteristics were outlined and discussed in Chapters 3 through 10.

- Successful caregivers are motivated by affection, responsibility, reciprocity, expectations of elders, obligation, and religion/spirituality.
- Successful caregivers have clearly defined roles and flexibility in their work schedules, thinking, and lifestyle.
- Successful caregivers try to control conflict and reduce stress to establish good family relationships.
- Successful caregivers have personalities that will promote psychological well-being and life-satisfaction.
- Successful caregivers use many strategies and adaptations to cope with the caregiving experience.
- Successful caregivers use their religious or spiritual beliefs while caregiving to help them cope with all aspects of caregiving.
- Successful caregivers know how to use extended help for respite care and intensive care.
- Successful caregivers have positive caregiving experiences because caregiving helps them fulfil many of their own needs, gain inner strength, and grow personally.

Successful caregiving should be part of the normal lifecycle. During one of my interviews, a wife had the following thoughts to share. "It's kind of a cycle. If one generation breaks the cycle by not being a caregiver, it's bad. It should be part of a person's heredity [or heritage]. That's how I feel." She was saying that we need to model caregiving to our children, so the process can continue generation after generation.

Are you still unsure of your final answer?

Here's my best shot!

When it comes to taking care of our elderly population, our society is not lacking in programs but clarity of purpose. As civilized people we need to ask ourselves

- What do we want to do with our elderly?
- Why would we want to do caregiving?
- How do we take care of elders in the most humane way?
- How much are we willing to sacrifice in terms of time, social life, and financial aid to do the right thing?

The *Graying of America* is here! It is no longer a future problem. We need to deal with this problem now. If we as adult children do not take care of our elders, the government will have to step in and take care of them. We can tuck them all neatly into institutions, or we can devise ways to take care of them ourselves, so we can reap some of the benefits of caregiving.

Taking care of our elderly parents should be an obligation felt by every adult child. One husband discussed this obligation in a thoughtful manner: "I don't think we're any different than anyone else when it comes to taking care of our parents. I think everyone is kind of obligated to their mom and dad when the time comes if they've [caregivers and elders] been on good terms." This husband felt it was important to stay on good terms with your parents so caregiving would be a positive experience. I think so, too.

The benefits for caregiving were stated throughout this book. The most prominent benefits were feeling good, peace of mind, spiritual growth, and learning how to deal with one's own aging process and mortality. The benefits by far outweigh the problems that might occur from caregiving.

The most humane way to deal with our elders is to take care of them ourselves. Common sense tells us that nobody can love, respect, and honor our parents like we can. *Don't expect others to give your parents the quality of care that you should be giving them.*

Taking care of our parents can mean sacrifices because caregiving takes a lot of time. It is very important to have a good network of help so you have some free time to yourself. There are many community and church people, service organizations, relatives, government programs, nursing homes, etc., that will help you with the tasks of caregiving.

Your social life could suffer, but who knows, you may develop a new social system that is also rewarding. One couple told me how their social life changed. A side benefit to doing caregiving for many years turned out to be a unique type of social life that is very rewarding for this couple. After a lifetime (since they married) of taking care of elderly parents (in and out of nursing homes) the wife had this to say: "I think ~ another thing ~ since we spent all our time at the nursing homes when we weren't working we didn't do anything else ~ but that's okay. Now that we're free, we are kind of lost when we don't have to go to the home."

This couple went on to explain how they had become friends with other caregivers, nursing home staff, and elderly residents of the home. Now that their parents had died, they still go to the home and visit these other friends and find this social activity very rewarding.

Costs for taking care of our elderly population, if they can't pay for themselves, will come out of our personal finances or we will pay more taxes to provide more government assistance for the elders who are in need. *Pay me now or pay me later* ~ it's all the same.

One last comment from a husband I interviewed might help you make the right choice: "If anyone reads this [the interview the couple gave me], and they are wondering if they should take on the responsibility of caregiving ~ I would strongly encourage it."

Are you still hesitating?

Go with your gut reaction! Give me your final answer!

Congratulations! You just won a million dollars worth of peace of mind that will promote the integrity you will need to enter the final stage of your own lifecycle.

Resources

Research

Erickson, M.E. (2001). Effects of motivation, roles, coping strategies, and adaptations in relationships and personality on caretaking of elderly parents by midlife couples. Ann Arbor, MI: UMI Dissertation Services.

Goldscheider, F.K., & Lawton, L. (1998). Family experiences and the erosion of support for intergenerational coresidence. Journal of Marriage and the Family, 60(3), 623-632.

Kramer, B.J. (1997). Gain in the caregiving experience: Where are we? What next? The Gerontologist, 37(2), 218-232.

Stone, D. (1999). Care and trembling. The American Prospect, 61(1), 61-67.

Stull, D.E., Cosbey, J., Bowman, K., & McNutt, W. (1997). Institutionalization: A continuation of family care. The Journal of Applied Gerontology, 16(4), 379-402.

U.S. Census Bureau Statistical Brief. (1995). Sixty-five plus in the United States. Economic and Statistic Administration, U.S. Department of Commerce, (pp. 1-8). http//www.census.gov/socdemo/www/agebrief

Sources

- AARP (American Association of Retired Persons), Washington, D.C.
- State Human Services
- Local Resource Directories
- Local County Social Services
- www.caregivingofelders

* There are many sources to contact for help and information. The sources listed here are a starting place.

Appendix
Research Procedures

I started planing and designing the research project that proceeded this book in 1999. A thorough review of caregiving literature helped me write the questionnaire, interview format, letter of query, and consent form needed to begin the interviews. Fifteen mid-life married couples in first or second marriages, who had shared a period of at least ten years together, were interviewed in rural Foster County, North Dakota. These couples were purposefully selected because they were likely to be knowledgeable and informative about caregiving. I made that assumption from personal knowledge I had about the people living in Foster County.

Couples were interviewed from March 2000 to November 2000. Personal contact was made with individuals in Foster county who had knowledge of couples who were now or had been doing caregiving of elderly parents. From the list of couples obtained from these informed sources, I contacted by phone the couples who met the eligibility requirements of my study. Of the 25 couples contacted via phone, 15 agreed to meet with me for interviews. After signing consent forms, the spouses each answered identical demographic questionnaires; then, the interviews began. Interviews lasted from 45 to 90 minutes. Interviews were tape recorded at the time they were taken, and transcribed at a later date. A checklist of behaviors observed during each interview was comprised after the interview was completed.

The reason I chose couples to interview was that I could not find any completed research that dealt specifically with couples working together to do caregiving. I wanted to see how married people worked together to provide caregiving for biological and in-law parents.

The four months after the interviews were spent analyzing the data. Interviews were read many times and coded. Information from each interview was put on a matrix of categories derived from the first interview. Data was then examined for similarities and differences between couples in each category. Clusters of comments were next put into categories and a matrix of categories, memos, notes and Ethnograph computer printouts were co-related. At the end, themes emerged from the interviews that make up the essential parts of the dissertation findings and also the chapters of this book.

Most of the quotes and data in this book come from the interviews done and the interpretation of the data. My own personal interpretations of the data and my own perceptions of the information gathered make up the material in this book. I make no attempt to develop generalizations about all caregiving couples, but rather I try to make sense of what 15 caregiving couples with positive attitudes about caregiving reported to me.